Supernatural Fragrance
Following the Perfume of His Virtue
by Steven Brooks

Supernatural Fragrance: Following the Perfume of His Virtue

Trilogy Christian Publishers A Wholly Owned Subsidiary of Trinity Broadcasting Network

2442 Michelle Drive Tustin, CA 92780

Copyright © 2021 by Steven Brooks

Rights Department, 2442 Michelle Drive, Tustin, CA 92780.

Trilogy Christian Publishing/TBN and colophon are trademarks of Trinity Broadcasting Network.

For information about special discounts for bulk purchases, please contact Trilogy Christian Publishing.

Trilogy Disclaimer: The views and content expressed in this book are those of the author and may not necessarily reflect the views and doctrine of Trilogy Christian Publishing or the Trinity Broadcasting Network.

Manufactured in the United States of America

10 9 8 7 6 5 4 3 2 1

Library of Congress Cataloging-in-Publication Data is available.

ISBN: 978-1-63769-486-2

E-ISBN: 978-1-63769-487-9

Endorsements

"Steven Brooks spoke for me on my tour to Israel. After he spoke, many, including myself, smelled the fragrance of lavender. Now it's God's time for all spiritual senses to be open. Steven has the authority to release this gift on you!"

Sid Israel Roth
Host, *It's Supernatural*

"Pastor Steven Brooks is a true friend and co-laborer in the kingdom of God who speaks as one who continually sits at the feet of our Master. His books and videos serve as edification to hungry souls, and they never fail to grant fresh heavenly perspectives (1 Corinthians 2:9-10).

"The *Supernatural Fragrance* of revelatory truths is Christocentric: they always point to the vivid beauty of Jesus. Let us consider the Song of Songs 4:6-7. The mountain of myrrh speaks of His death at Calvary, while the hill of frankincense represents His resurrection from death. Through His death and resurrection, holy fragrance has been lavished on the body of Christ as we who are called to be His own are crucified with Him, now seated with our resurrected Lord in the heavenly places (Romans 6:6; Ephesians 2:6; 2 Corinthians 2:14).

"*Supernatural Fragrance* is unequivocally one of the most profound and empowering books on this little-explored subject. It is a must-read for anyone who endeavors to be perfumed with the aroma of Christ (Song of Songs 1:3-4). Pastor Steven has drawn upon his wealth of spiritual insights and penned down seventy-seven different fragrances and their associated spiritual meanings. Beyond that, he gives the reader a roadmap to their practical applications. It is clear that his desire is for the reader to augment our spiritual sense of smell to enrich our kingdom walk. I am confident this book will be a perennial classic in the library of all of us who yearn deeply for the sweet scent of His presence.

Jedidiah Tham
Living Lilies Ministry, Singapore

"It is my joy to encourage your reading of this wonderful book, which I have found to be so amazing and new. Did not the Lord say that new wine should be poured into new skins? His wine and its smell always require new skins. Steven's books are demanding in this regard: they ask that whatever our age, our skins be always new to welcome the gifts of the Spirit, those gifts that he makes us discover. This time we are invited, for our joy, to follow the wake of the perfume. May many readers follow the path of the odor! In doing so, they will be sanctified."

Father Geoffroy de Lestrange
Roman Catholic priest, France

"In this ground-breaking book, Pastor Steven Brooks shows us that the 'odor of sanctity,' known from many of the great saints of the church, can be an experience for all of us along our pilgrim way. We can participate in 'discernment of spirits' through smell, even as we live lives exuding the fragrance of Christ, the Anointed One. This spiritual perception is no mere religious curiosity but a serious piece of our armament in spiritual warfare and a source of refreshment and consolation amidst all of life's varied experiences. We can smell victory and triumph and the freshness of the kingdom, which is more real and vibrant than the freshest days on earth. After absorbing the message of this book, the fruit of Steven's meticulous research and personal experience, one may never take the sense of smell for granted again. Smell may be more than a physical sense; it has the potential to be the organ of prophetic and spiritual insight."

Dr. Ronald Thomas
PhD, University of Cambridge, United Kingdom
Associate professor of theology
Belmont Abbey College
Belmont, North Carolina

Dedication

Supernatural Fragrance is dedicated to Saint Padre Pio (May 25, 1887–September 23, 1968). Padre Pio was a Capuchin friar and priest within the Catholic Church. For over fifty years, he functioned in the ministry office of a prophet and touched countless lives around the world. With Padre Pio, it was said that the extraordinary was ordinary, the uncommon was common, and the supernatural was natural. He turned many to the Lord through his prayers and his usage of the gifts of the Spirit, such as the word of knowledge, prophecy, and working of miracles. Those who had the joy of seeing him minister at Mass often described a heavenly fragrance that would diffuse through the air. This "aroma of paradise" seemed to emanate from the padre and would manifest in many different scents to those who were around him, although he himself was unaware of it. While many experienced these fragrances in the padre's presence, it would also happen to those who were hundreds of miles away from him, and it even continued to occur after his death as a supernatural sign of a prayer being answered or a blessing being released. God certainly anointed him with a miracle ministry. However, he also lived a very normal life displayed through his humor, common sense, and authentic behavior, which at times included his gruffness when dealing with certain stubborn people who were slow to repent and soften their hearts toward the ways of God. His ministry and legacy continue to inspire those who are faithful to Christ. Approximately eight million pilgrims come each year to San Giovanni Rotondo, where Padre Pio lived and is now buried.

Contents

First the Natural, Then the Supernatural

> So the last Adam is a life-giving Spirit. But we should notice that the order is "natural" first and then "spiritual". The first man came out of the earth, a material creature. The second man came from Heaven and was the Lord himself. For the life of this world men are made like the material man; but for the life that is to come they are made like the one from Heaven. So that just as we have been made like the material pattern, so we shall be made like the Heavenly pattern.
>
> 1 Corinthians 15:46-49 (Phillips)

In these verses, we see that Paul is referring to the way in which God reveals divine secrets through the natural realm. What you experience in the natural is an indicator of the reality of that same experience in the spiritual realm, where it has a deeper and fuller expression. In the context of his statement, Paul is referring to our natural body. Because we have a natural body, it should be easy to understand that we also have a spiritual body. There is always a parallel between the natural realm and the spiritual realm. If you can smell in the natural, then you can also smell in the spiritual. If you are able to see in the natural, you can also see in the spiritual.

There are five basic human senses, which are sight, taste, touch, hearing, and smell. Our sense of smell is used constantly. This book will take you on an explorative journey into the sensory realm of smell that exists in the spiritual world. As a Christian, your inheritance in Christ qualifies you not only for the natural but also for the supernatural. We should become acquainted with both realms because we are called by God to live in each of them. Just as on the earth you can own two homes, as a believer, you have two inheritances, the natural and spiritual. As the possessor of two houses, you own keys to both; therefore, you can go in and out anytime you want. It is always best to have an understanding of the natural first, and then we can be equipped with information that helps us progress more effectively into the spiritual. In light of this, let's consider the natural world of smell.

Each day we encounter different kinds of smells. Some things have a foul and unpleasant odor. Whether it's taking out the kitchen trash or washing dirty laundry, we try to get past disagreeable smells as quickly as possible. Other things emit a pleasing fragrance that brings a smile on our face and causes us to linger in their presence. By definition, the word fragrance means a pleasing or delicate odor that gives off a sweet or pleasant smell, such as fresh flowers or perfume.

Fragrance is all around us. A few decades ago, scientists thought that smell was on a level of importance much lower than our other physical senses, such as vision or hearing. However, we now understand that smell is critical to the way we live our lives, and it has a huge impact on the quality of our lives. There are so many things that our nose is able to discern that our other senses can't evaluate nearly as well. For example, you may want to buy fish at the grocery store so that you can take it home and prepare it for dinner. While at the store, you first visually examine the fish as an indicator of freshness. You can look closely at the eyes of the fish to see if they are clear and not glazed or cloudy. Clear eyes denote freshness in fish, but if they are glazed over, it means the fish has been there longer than preferred. You can take your finger and feel the fish, gently pushing against the areas with the most flesh. A feeling of firmness is a good indicator of freshness. If the fish is soft and mushy, then it's not going to taste very good.

But concerning fish, what is the number one judgment we use to conclude whether it is truly fresh or not? It's the smell of the fish. Simply put, if the fish smells fishy, then it is not fresh, and you should probably choose something else for dinner. Fish that are fresh have no smell. The other day Kelly and I walked into a large grocery store. The seafood section was in the far back of the store, at least one hundred feet away. As soon as we entered through the front of the sliding glass doors, we were greeted with the overpowering smell of old fish. We both looked at each other and said, "Their seafood is not fresh." We knew that without needing to visit their seafood display for verification.

If you wake up in the morning and decide to have cereal for breakfast, what do you do if you notice the expiration date on your milk carton is passed? You could possibly throw away the carton in the trash, but you also don't want to waste the milk if it is still good. So what do you do to discern freshness? Do you *touch* the milk to make sure it feels fresh? Or do you put your ear next to the carton in order to *hear* the milk before drinking it? No, you open the lid and *smell* it. Your nose is the final authority for how you base your decision. *Your nose knows!* If it smells fresh, then it is most likely still good to drink for another day or so. Therefore, you ignore the expiration date on the carton, and you sit down and enjoy your breakfast.

I grew up on a farm as a young boy, and we had a large garden that produced countless fresh vegetables. In some ways, this was wonderful because I liked many of the things we harvested, such as strawberries and cantaloupes, but in other ways, I didn't like it because we had to eat whatever we grew, and I didn't always like what my parents had planted. For some reason, Brussels sprouts and okra were often grown, and they would eventually end up at the dinner table. When it came to cooking the vegetables we ate, they weren't fried but boiled in water, so my two brothers and I always got the full factor of the flavor and texture of various foods during mealtime. To me, boiled okra has a particularly slimy sensation when you eat it.

Although it was a struggle for me to chew it because I considered it to be an unpleasant-tasting vegetable, I could eventually get it down. But for some reason, the dreaded Brussels sprouts were almost unbearable to my taste buds. Today, I know many people who love eating them, but I've never liked the way they tasted, and as a kid, I got an instant gag reflex from the flavor and smell of them. Quite a few times, I was able to secretly slip a few Brussels sprouts off of my plate and hand them to our family dog, who lay beneath the table as we ate our evening meal. But eventually, I think my father caught on, and he wanted me to be a good boy and finish my food. My mother was always there to encourage me to eat everything on my plate while reminding me that there were starving children in China who had no food and that I should be grateful to God for my generous serving of Brussels sprouts. I told my mother that I wished to send my Brussels sprouts to China as an offering to feed the poor, but she didn't seem to take my idea with much seriousness.

Through the mysterious grace of God, I discovered during one particular evening meal that if I pinched my nose and held it firmly closed when I ate my food that I couldn't taste what I was eating. This funny trick helped me survive my tribulation days of okra, cauliflower, collard greens, spinach, and the dreaded Brussels sprouts. What we recognize as the taste of our food is not just the work of our taste buds. Your sense of smell has a direct relation to how the food you eat tastes. God designed us so that our noses have the ability to detect around 20,000 different odors. You are able to place that huge list of odors within about ten different fields of intensity. Scientists tell us that smell is detected through your nose and mouth when chewing food. They say when you can't smell through your nose, your ability to taste food is greatly diminished. (I could have told them that through my discovery at the dinner table as a young boy living in the back woods of Mississippi.) If you've ever had a severe cold with your nose stopped up, then you know what I'm talking about. Without smell, there isn't any taste.

If you want to personally experience eating without tasting, you can do a simple test. Get some jelly beans of various flavors, and select three primary flavors, such as apple, cherry, or licorice. Pinch your nose so that you can't breathe in or out, and put a jelly bean into your mouth. Chew it up completely and swallow it. Then, take a drink of water and swish it around in your mouth and then swallow it also. Now let go of your nose. You'll notice that you never tasted the jelly bean regardless of what the flavor was. Now, put a jelly bean into your mouth and chew it with your nose open, and you'll be back to enjoying the normal full flavor experience.

If you're really adventurous about wanting to know how your taste is influenced by smell, then try taking one apple and one onion. Peel an onion and cut it in half. Next, take a crisp apple and cut it in half. Make sure you remove the core from the apple along with any seeds. Now close your eyes and pinch your nose firmly shut. With your eyes closed, have someone pass you either the apple or the onion without them telling you which one you are receiving. Take it and eat it, and you'll discover that you can't tell the difference in taste between the two.

Understanding how the body responds to smell could potentially help someone who may wish to shed a few extra pounds lose weight. If you want to lose weight, then do your best to avoid the smells of your favorite foods. Just driving by a steakhouse and smelling the meat cooking can initiate an appetite in some people. Cookies and fresh bread baking in the oven can be heavenly in smell and can also easily activate a desire to eat even when you're not hungry. By not smelling food, it becomes a little more manageable to not eat. However, we know this is far easier said than done when it comes to avoiding the smell of food. But at least knowing how your body responds to the different smells of food can be helpful at certain times when trying to apply the brakes of self-control and not overeat.

Life offers many simple pleasures that can bring a smile. When traveling, it's refreshing to check into a hotel and see an elegant floral display in the lobby. The color and fragrance create a soothing and comforting feeling, helping you relax and be happy when away from home. Such experiences also create pleasant memories so that in the future you will want to return there again. Even when on an airplane, what a difference it makes in your travel perspective of the airline and your mood when you go to use the lavatory, and there you discover a real flower in a wall-mounted vase placed near the sink by a caring and thoughtful flight attendant. I've had that happen several times on international flights, but it, unfortunately, seems to have become a rare thing nowadays.

Fragrance makes everything in life better, which is why many people choose to wear perfume. Beautiful perfumes can be mesmerizing, even intoxicating. This proved extremely helpful during the fifteenth century when the accepted understanding amongst Europeans was that baths were dangerous to health. King Louis XIV (1638–1715) is reported to have only taken three baths in his lifetime. In that era of time, they thought bathing in warm water would spread disease and make you susceptible to the plague. Because of this widespread mindset, the vast majority of the lower classes of society completely abandoned taking baths. King Louis constantly wore heavy amounts of perfume in a valiant attempt to cover up his body odor, but his efforts appear to have fallen short. The Russian ambassador to France wrote that King Louis "stunk like a wild animal."[1]

The French military leader Napoleon Bonaparte was captivated by fine cologne. Historians say he wore one gallon of perfume each day; he used it in his water when washing and would drench his shoulders and neck with it. He especially loved the scent of rosemary and jasmine. Records from 1810 show that he ordered 144 bottles of cologne for himself from Chardin, his perfumer. In 1812, he ordered 108 cases of cologne, with six bottles in each case! He would often place such large orders for cologne every four months.[2] Today, this type of usage would certainly be considered excessive and definitely not a good idea in a confined space, such as being on a packed airplane during a crowded holiday season. While the universal rule of wearing perfume is "soft attracts, strong offends," I can nevertheless appreciate Napoleon's passion for a well-crafted fragrance and his desire to completely eliminate any unpleasant body odors in an era before deodorant was invented. The French have been world leaders in the perfume industry for a long time, and they still set a high standard for others to emulate.

When we consider the world of fragrance as expressed through perfume, many are aware of what is considered to be the most famous perfume in the world, which is Chanel No. 5. There is no other perfume that has reached the same level of iconic status as this classic perfume, which is known for its clean and floral fragrance. Coco Chanel, a French businesswoman and Parisian socialite, launched the perfume in 1921 with a desire to have a "woman's perfume with a woman's scent." Some of the key notes in Chanel No. 5 are jasmine, rose, ylang-ylang, iris, amber, patchouli, sandalwood, and vanilla. This fragrance is considered to be the first perfume to combine multiple scents in a time when perfumes basically featured only a single flower for their scent.

Ernest Beaux (1881–1961)

The master perfumer that Coco Chanel commissioned to create her famous perfume was a man named Ernest Beaux, who lived in Grasse, France, which, at that time, was the capital of the world's perfume industry. After several months of work, he developed ten samples that he presented to her, and when she smelled sample No. 5, she immediately knew that it was going to be a revolutionary perfume unlike anything else the world had known. Chanel No. 5 was a barrier breaker in the perfume industry. It was one of the first perfumes to be created with synthetics. The true secret of Chanel No. 5's success is its tiny molecules called aldehydes, which have been synthesized in a laboratory. Aldehydes are organic compounds of carbon, oxygen, and hydrogen. They can be worked with in a laboratory and taken through a chemical process where it's possible to isolate a certain scent. Aldehydes are aroma boosters, acting on fragrances in a similar way that seasoning acts on the foods we eat. Several years before Ernest Beaux created his famous perfume, he took a trip to the Arctic Circle during the time of the midnight sun. His visit coincided with the time when the lakes and rivers release a natural perfume of extreme freshness. In his mind, Beaux was able to somehow memorize that sensory experience. When consigned by Coco Chanel to create an extraordinary fragrance, he was able through much effort to replicate in his laboratory that memorable "Arctic" fragrance with aldehydes. It is the "Arctic" scent in Chanel No. 5 that gives the perfume its soft punch of cleanness.[3]

While some people may be prejudiced against synthetics in their favor of all-natural products, there are actually many benefits to using synthetics in perfume. One of their greatest strengths is that synthetics allow a master perfumer to have a tremendous range of scents. Your palette of scents to work with becomes literally unlimited with synthetics. You can combine scents of vanilla with sky, rose with chocolate, roasted coffee beans with leather, or caramel with salt water. One popular synthetic fragrance a few years ago was that of french fries from a certain fast-food hamburger restaurant. It sounds crazy, but countless teenagers loved it. Some synthetics are edible, so it's possible you could take out your perfume spritzer and spray onto your arms the scent of french fries and then lick it off later when you became hungry for lunch.

Synthetics are also easier to manufacture than natural products, and they can be reproduced more consistently from lot to lot. It also helps save certain trees that are quickly shrinking in number due to overexploitation. The East Indian sandalwood tree is prized for its aromatic heartwood and natural oils. There is an annual global demand of 200 tons of sandalwood oil from this particular tree, with its high demand primarily coming from China. Pure sandalwood oil sells for $3,000 for thirty ounces. Even the tree's waste chippings left over from the distilled extraction process sell for $1,000 per ton, mainly to be used for incense sticks. Five hundred million (500,000,000) incense sticks are burned every day in India. Synthetics allow the need for fewer trees to be cut down by allowing the same scent to be made in a laboratory. Because of Chanel No.

5, almost all modern perfumes use some measure of synthetics to achieve their complex scents. This is also true for the widely popular Angel perfume created by Thierry Mugler, which uses the synthetic known as ethyl maltol, the same molecule found in the intoxicatingly sweet smell of cotton candy.

Legend has it that Chanel No. 5 was actually created by an unintentional laboratory accident. The story is that Ernest Beaux had an assistant who was going to use a diluted aldehyde for the Chanel No. 5 mix, but by mistake, he grabbed a bottle that was the full-strength mixture and added it instead. The huge dose of aldehyde was what jolted the perfume compound into its incredible finished product. The results were epic, and the rest was history in the making. Over the following years, Ernest Beaux went on to create some of the most respected perfumes in the industry before retiring in 1954. He passed away in June 1961. The church in which his funeral was held was completely decorated in roses.

Dr. Wade Taylor (1924–2012)

A close and dear minister friend of mine, Dr. Wade Taylor, once described to me a mighty outpouring of the Holy Spirit that took place at a Bible college that he was attending in the late 1950s. He said the glory of God was so strong in the revival that there was a constant manifestation of heavenly fragrance. He described it as being like someone was taking gallons and gallons of Chanel No. 5 and pouring it into the meeting room. The fragrance that filled the room was both beautiful and intense. At one point in the revival, he said a "fountain of new wine" spiritually appeared in the center of the room. Although you could not see it with your physical eyes, you could, however, place your hands into the fountain and "throw" it onto others. Being splashed with the new wine caused a release of laughter and overflowing joy to break forth upon those touched by it. The smell of "new wine" was profuse around the fountain area.

In the same way, it is also possible for us to encounter the Lord Jesus through spiritual fragrance, which is miraculous in its manifestation. Several years before Dr. Taylor went to be with the Lord, he laid his hands upon me and released his prophetic mantle to me with his intent that the type of supernatural encounters he experienced would continue through my life and ministry. God is now moving forward with bold and extravagant expressions of His love and blessing for His people through supernatural fragrance. He is also graciously reaching out to those who aren't yet well acquainted with Him in these areas of the supernatural. Through prophetic encounters that are orchestrated by the Holy Spirit, God is opening up the realm of the invisible to many who are being allowed to see, hear, and smell the glories of heaven. You will see that just as your nose knows in the natural, your nose will also know in the spiritual.

The first supernatural fragrance that manifested in my life happened in November 1995 when Kelly and I were together. We had just met a few days earlier, and we were still getting to know each other. We attended a prophetic conference hosted by a local prophet. After this minister concluded his message, he began to walk around, laying hands on people and prophesying over them. Many of those in attendance had gotten out of their chairs and had gathered toward the front, including both Kelly and me. The prophet walked toward Kelly and me, and when he got near us, he put one hand on my head and one hand on Kelly's head and spoke a blessing over us. When he did this, Kelly and I both gently fell to the floor as we were overcome by the presence of the Lord. The moment we fell on the floor, we both were encompassed in a thick but invisible cloud of frankincense. We just laid there for a few minutes and enjoyed the moment. The presence of the Lord was very strong, and the beautiful aroma of frankincense kept swirling around us. We were married two months later.

Frankincense represents that you are standing (or laying) in a portal between earth and heaven, and God is releasing His best blessing into your life. He brought Kelly into my life to be my wife, the perfect person for me. When this fragrance occurs, I would encourage you to ask the Holy Spirit what specific blessing is being released to you.

The second time I smelled a supernatural fragrance was when Kelly and I were together in a service in which an old Pentecostal preacher was ministering. When he finished preaching, he sat down in a chair on the platform and announced that the Holy Spirit would now begin to move all throughout the audience and manifest supernatural fragrances. He was obviously a man of faith because when he announced this, nothing had yet happened that could be considered supernatural. But as soon as he finished speaking, immediately, all over the meeting hall with about 800 people present, fragrances of all sorts began to pop up everywhere. About two inches below my nose, it seemed as if someone had taken a bucket of grape juice and fully splashed it before me. As people would joyfully shout out what they were smelling, he would give the prophetic interpretation of that particular smell. I loudly said, "Grape juice!" Having heard me, he replied saying grape juice represents the joy of the Lord, which comes from drinking the new wine of the Holy Spirit. Decades later, I'm still drinking the new wine and I'm still full of joy!

Sitting next to me on my right was Kelly, and she encountered the pleasing fragrance of evergreen. Over the years now, she often gets the evergreen scent when prayerfully seeking God's perfect will in specific areas. Evergreen speaks of being seated with Christ in the high places and being able to see with prophetic eagle-type vision. Since these initial discoveries of spiritual smell, there have been countless others that followed. The scents have had tremendous variation, with some of them being pleasing and others being awful, each distinct spiritual smell carrying a clear meaning that corresponds with the natural world in which we live.

As you study the pages of this book, I ask that you will open your heart to God's prophetic language that is expressed through supernatural fragrances. I believe the Lord will introduce and immerse you into this biblical form of divine communication. This knowledge will allow you to be more discerning and effective in determining the direction that God has for you to go in. In the next chapter, I explain the meaning of many of the most commonly occurring heavenly fragrances. It is my desire to see this gift blossom in your life so that you may enjoy all of the good things that God has made available for you.

Supernatural Fragrances Listed and Their Meanings

Over the years, Kelly and I have experienced countless supernatural fragrances that have manifested in our meetings and also in our personal lives. When the gift of working of miracles combined with the gift of discerning of spirits is in operation, we not only smell these fragrances, but others begin to smell them too. There are times when it's not unusual for everyone present to smell in the spirit realm: this includes believers and even unbelievers who have not confessed faith in Christ.

It has been well said that God's healing power is the fruitful vine that grows over the church wall and reaches into the world of sinners and unbelievers. I have a relative that I visit from time to time. He has a beautiful backyard where we sometimes go for a nice barbeque. His backyard is fenced-in and directly adjoins his neighbor's backyard. A six-foot-tall wooden fence separates their two properties. The neighbor has a large orange tree at the back of his property, and its branches have grown over the fence and extend within easy reach for us on our side of the fence. So, whenever I visit, I always walk over and grab an orange or two from the branch and eat them while waiting for the barbeque grill to become ready for cooking. This is perfectly acceptable (and legal) for me to do because his branch has grown over the wall and is now on my relative's property. However, I am not allowed to climb over the fence and enter into his backyard and gather oranges without permission; that would be a form of trespassing. In His love and mercy, God allows the gifts of the Holy Spirit to reach over the fence of the church in order to soften the hearts of those who are lost in sin and draw them to salvation. He can manifest His power toward them through various signs, wonders, and miracles such as supernatural fragrances, which give validity to the gospel message.

In this chapter, I list some of the fragrances we have smelled, along with their prophetic meaning. Most of these fragrances we have encountered many times, and they are consistent in their meaning. Keep in mind that a fragrance can have more than one symbolic meaning simply because we have all had various life experiences. The way in which we interpret things can be influenced by the country or state we grew up in as well as the location, such as in the city or a rural area. Interpreting fragrance can be similar to interpreting a God-given dream. The content of most dreams is 95 percent symbolic. Since very few dreams are literal, the others are going to need an interpretation in order to be understood. There are basic, common denominators based on Scripture and the natural world in which we live that can be applied when it comes to unraveling biblical numerology, apocalyptic symbols, dream interpretation, and especially supernatural fragrances. While there can be some variation in the prophetic and symbolic meaning of a fragrance, I think you will discover over time and through experience that the core interpretation presented here is on target.

Some of the fragrances listed are beautiful in their aroma; others are awful. In the end times, it will become critical to discern the works of the enemy. Throughout biblical history, smell has always been the physical symbol of discernment. We see this revealed in the Song of Solomon: "Your neck is like an ivory tower. Your eyes are the pools of Heshbon by the gate of Bath Rabbim. Your nose is like the tower of Lebanon looking toward Damascus" (Song of Solomon 7:4).

The nose being like the tower of Lebanon is a representation of the tower's defensive structure designed for protection against the enemy. The tower (the nose) looking toward Damascus indicates the ancient (and modern-day) enemy of Israel, which is Syria, whose capital is Damascus. This symbolizes that through our nose, we can discern the movements of the enemy and be on our guard. It is the mature Christian who can discern between the genuine and the counterfeit. Therefore be open to any fragrance that the Holy Spirit allows you to supernaturally smell, even if it is unpleasant, as some disturbing fragrances are meant to highlight your need to be cautious and extra alert.

This has been a journey of discovery for me over the years to unlock the meaning of spiritual fragrances. When people smell these fragrances in my meetings, the first thing they want to know is what the specific smell represents. In other words, what message God is trying to speak to them through that particular scent. Here is my interpretation of various supernatural fragrances that I have compiled to aid you in understanding their symbolic meaning.

Amber. Amber represents an open door for visions and being caught up in the throne room of God.

> Then I looked, and there was a likeness, like the appearance of fire—from the appearance of His waist and downward, fire; and from His waist and upward, like the appearance of brightness, like the color of amber.
>
> Ezekiel 8:2

Apple Pie. Freedom, love for America; it can also mean there is something good for you at home.

"Now the Lord is the Spirit, and where the Spirit of the Lord is, there is freedom" (2 Corinthians 3:17, NIV).

Ashes. Your sins are burned up, gone, and forgotten. Don't go back to the past. Some years back, I was ministering in Calgary, Alberta, Canada, when the Holy Spirit began to move very strongly in the meeting. The keyboard player was softly playing on the keyboard as I ministered. We began to smell the supernatural smell of smoke, and then suddenly, the keyboard player watched as, before his eyes, the top of his keyboard became covered with real ashes. Overcome by the presence of the Lord, he gently fell backward and off the small bench he was sitting on. He lay on the floor for quite some time. It was a supernatural sign to him from God that all of his sins were like ashes, similar to the whole burnt offering God required of the Israelites. In the old covenant system of offerings, after the sin offering was made, the only thing left after it was burnt up was ashes, a symbolic reference to the atoning work that Jesus accomplished for us while on the cross.

"I will never again remember their sins and lawless deeds" (Hebrews 10:17b, NLT).

"Then the priest will burn the entire sacrifice on the altar as a burnt offering. It is a special gift, a pleasing aroma to the LORD" (Leviticus 1:9b, NLT).

Baby Powder. A comforting word. Often when I minister and hold a microphone, it will begin to smell like baby powder. This is the Holy Spirit letting me know that I am to comfort the Lord's people with a soothing word that strengthens them and refreshes them. At one point in my ministry, an esteemed minister of the Lord noted for operating in the gift of working of miracles, Dr. Gary Greenwald, gave me his very nice coat after having concluded a meal together. He said, "As you put it on, let it be as a new mantle to you, from me." To my surprise, the collar of the coat suddenly began to emit the fragrance of baby powder (which represents soothing comfort and freshness) and frankincense (a sign that you are receiving a special blessing). Other ministers at the dinner table noticed the pleasing fragrance of baby powder exuding from the coat and marveled at the supernatural wonder which the Lord had done. Recently I went to bed late at night after having spent several hours in uninterrupted prayer. As I got into the bed and laid down, my wife said, "Steven, the smell of baby powder is strongly coming from you." There will always be a need for God's servants to be anointed so that we may bring a fresh word from the Lord that comforts and delivers those who are in distressing situations.

"Comfort, comfort my people, says your God" (Isaiah 40:1, NIV).

Barbeque. The release of the rhema word, feeding people with the savory meat of God's Word. This smell can become intense in a meeting, especially when the Word of God is taught to those who have not had a good spiritual meal in a long time and are very hungry. It became so strong once when I ministered in a meeting in New York that church members began looking inside and outside of the church to see who was cooking the delicious barbeque. Yet, the smell was coming from within the sanctuary where the teaching was taking place. Nobody was cooking any form of meat or food in the natural.

"When the LORD your God has enlarged your territory as he promised you, and you crave meat and say, 'I would like some meat,' then you may eat as much of it as you want" (Deuteronomy 12:20, NIV).

Bleach. Deep cleansing from evil spirits.

"The seventy-two returned with joy, saying, 'Lord, even the demons are subject to us in your name'" (Luke 10:17, ESV).

Blueberries. Ability to see visions, to see in the spirit. The color blue represents the prophetic; blue skies relate to the open heaven. Blueberries look similar in shape to the human eye, and blueberries contain an antioxidant called anthocyanin which has been shown in Japanese studies to help reduce eye strain and improve vision.[4] Often this scent can also be an indicator that God's healing anointing is present to heal the sick.

> Then Elisha prayed and said, "O Lord, please open his eyes that he may see." So the Lord opened the eyes of the young man, and he saw, and behold, the mountain was full of horses and chariots of fire all around Elisha.
>
> 2 Kings 6:17 (ESV)

Bouquet of the Lake. Seer and prophetic anointing, also the mystic saint anointing produced through much time spent alone with God. This fragrance is the signature scent of Benoite Rencurel. It is a beautiful floral mixture that contains the combined fragrances of Jesus, Mary, the mother of Jesus, various angels, and that of Benoite herself. Benoite lived in the seventeenth century in Laus, France. Laus means "lake" in the local dialect. Her father died when she was seven, and she became a shepherdess at the age of twelve. She had no education and never learned to read or write. At the age of seventeen, she began to have visions from the Holy Spirit in which Mary, the mother of Jesus, would appear to her. The gospel message contained within these visions would soon greatly affect the area, with many people receiving salvation in Christ and physical healing. Benoite was highly developed in the gift of discerning of spirits. She taught that the fragrances of the angelic hierarchy have as much variation as the perfume of flowers. She said that the fragrances of our Lord Jesus Christ surpass in an infinite degree every other fragrance. While still on the earth, Benoite was greatly known for the fragrances that emitted from within her, which were said to be easily perceived even from a great distance. When she would have heavenly visions, the perfume would be so potent that it was said to be overpowering. This supernatural perfume on her caused those near her to be deeply touched with the love of God. She died a few days after Christmas in 1718 at the age of seventy-one. When she passed away, the entire valley of Laus was flooded with a pleasant perfume.[5] Even today, the "bouquet of the lake" fragrance is still perceived by many pilgrims who visit Laus, France.

"Awake, north wind, and come, south wind! Blow on my garden, that its fragrance may spread everywhere. Let my beloved come into his garden and taste its choice fruits" (Song of Solomon 4:16, NIV).

Bubble Gum. Behaving as an immature Christian.

"He is the one we proclaim, admonishing and teaching everyone with all wisdom, so that we may present everyone fully mature in Christ" (Colossians 1:28, NIV).

Burning Wood. Cleansing, removing of a wrong priority or focus.

The fire will show if a person's work has any value. If the work survives, that builder will receive a reward. But if the work is burned up, the builder will suffer great loss. The builder will be saved, but like someone barely escaping through a wall of flames.

1 Corinthians 3:13a-14 (NLT)

Butterscotch. A sweetness that comes from being together in unity with other believers in Christ.

Behold, how good and pleasant it is when brothers dwell in unity! It is like the precious oil on the head, running down on the beard, on the beard of Aaron, running down on the collar of his robes!

Psalm 133:1-2 (ESV)

Cedar. Clarity of mind, mental brilliance, operating in the mind of Christ, thinking like a king.

> So Solomon built the temple and finished it. He lined its interior walls with cedar boards, paneling them from the floor of the temple to the ceiling. The inside of the temple was cedar, carved with ornamental buds and open flowers. All was cedar; there was no stone to be seen.
>
> 1 Kings 6:14, 15a, 18

Cherry Scented Pipe Tobacco. This "grandfather" type of fragrance represents God spending time with His children. It can also manifest if you have grandchildren and you are enjoyably spending time with them.

"Grandchildren are the crown of the aged, and the glory of children is their fathers" (Proverbs 17:6, ESV).

Chocolate. Angels are present, and something good is going to happen to you. You may not be able to see them, but they are near you. It also speaks of being satisfied.

"Do not forget to entertain strangers, for by so doing some have unwittingly entertained angels" (Hebrews 13:2).

Cigarette smoke. Instant deliverance from cigarettes and other nicotine-related addictions. Once I ministered in a church in southern California. As I walked up to the pulpit to begin my teaching, I was overwhelmed with the smell of cigarette smoke, but no one was smoking in the building. I asked if anyone would like to get delivered from cigarettes and for them to come to the front, and I told them that Jesus would set them free. There were lots of men in business suits and ladies nicely dressed. I thought that perhaps two or three people would come forward. To my surprise, almost the entire church stood up and began to come toward the platform where I was standing. They threw their cigarette packs on the altar, completely covering the altar area. As I prayed for them, the Lord Jesus broke the enemy's grip on their lives in this area, and they were set free.

"The Spirit of the Lord is on Me, because He has anointed Me [...] to proclaim freedom to the captives and to set free the oppressed" (Luke 4:18a, c; HCSB).

Cinnamon. Purity and commissioning by God for your assignment. Angels can also be sent from heaven, bringing with them "heavenly fire" they touch you with. Smelling and tasting cinnamon on the tongue represents a deeper calling into the prophetic and cleansing from the world.

> Then one of the seraphim flew to me, having in his hand a live coal which he had taken with the tongs from the altar. And he touched my mouth with it, and said: "Behold, this has touched your lips; Your iniquity is taken away, And your sin purged."
>
> Isaiah 6:6-7

Citronella. Immunity against the attacks of the enemy that would drain the life out of you. This fragrance is often used in bug sprays and candles to ward off mosquitos.

Mosquitos usually come out strongest at sunset. This fragrance will often manifest to those who are older in life (their sunset years) as an encouragement to stay fully devoted to the Lord, making their time count and doing all they can to be involved in the Lord's work. This fragrance also carries with it the Lord's intent for that person to expect the blessing of health and longevity to rest upon them as long as they continue to serve Him.

"They shall still bear fruit in old age; They shall be fresh and flourishing" (Psalm 92:14).

Cloves. Protection from all forms of disease as well as protection from theft and loss. Clove oil was the primary oil worn in France by a legendary group of four thieves in the Medieval Ages during the Bubonic plague. The thieves were originally spice traders who made their living by importing spices from India. Unable to do business due to the plague, the men turned to thievery, stripping the dead of jewelry and valuables. However, they never got infected with the highly contagious bacteria because they were drenched in clove oil and a mixture of other types of oil that are highly antiseptic.

"Look, I have given you the authority to trample on snakes and scorpions and over all the power of the enemy; nothing will ever harm you" (Luke 10:19, HCSB).[6]

Coffee. Wake up, pay attention, and be spiritually alert. This is often a call to be engaged in early morning prayer.

> O God, You are my God;
>
> Early will I seek You;
>
> My soul thirsts for You;
>
> My flesh longs for You
>
> In a dry and thirsty land
>
> Where there is no water.
>
> Psalm 63:1

Cookies. The cookie fragrance represents the blessings of God and that God wants you to take a cookie (a blessing) by faith. The Lord can be quite insistent with this because so few of His people actually eat His cookies. His blessings include health, blessed relationships, finances, heart's desires, and much more. About ten years ago, I one day laid down on the couch in the living room to take a nap in the afternoon. I was awakened to the very loud and distinct sound of someone eating something that was crunchy. The crunching sound was actually so loud that I could tell it was being supernaturally amplified as the sound appeared to fill my entire house. When I had opened my eyes and sat about halfway up, I clearly saw in a vision Jesus standing at the end of the couch eating a cookie. He smiled at me, and although He didn't speak, He conveyed the thought that He wanted me to take a cookie. Over the years, I have learned to be sensitive to the cookie fragrance. Recently I had a desire to purchase something that appealed to me. I went to the local store that carries this product and inquired if it was in stock. The salesman said, "No, it's not in stock. It appears you and many others want one of these. At this time, no one has it in stock, and there's no telling how long it will be before we ever get another one in the store." I went home and checked on the internet to see if there was anywhere in the nation where this item could be purchased. Out of the multitudes of retail stores and online sites that carry this particular product, there was not a single store in the country that had it in stock. I went before the Lord in prayer concerning this, and I said to God, "Heavenly Father, that item is my cookie, and I believe You will cause one of them to come into stock here at my local store." Each passing day I reminded the Lord in prayer that He was well able to bring me my cookie and that I was confident He would do it. One week later, I went back to the store and inquired again if they had received one in stock. The salesman said, "No, we still don't have a _____ in stock." (He spoke the particular model out loud.) When he said this, a young saleswoman who just happened to be walking past us overheard what he told me and said, "Oh, we just got one of those in this morning. It was just delivered here." Some of the sales team went into the back receiving area to check, and there it was, unopened, brand new, factory-sealed, and loaded with every possible option. With astonishment, they brought it out to me. When I saw it, I joyfully shouted, "I'll take it!" I then immediately paid for it on the spot. People in major cities across America desperately wanted to purchase this item, but it was unavailable. Yet God sent one to me at a local store only three miles from my house in the small town of North Wilkesboro, North Carolina, with a population of only 4,225 people. All of the sweet blessings of God are accessed by faith. When you smell the cookie fragrance or get touched with the "cookie anointing," use your faith and get your cookie.

"Jesus said to her, 'Did I not say to you that if you would believe you would see the glory of God?'" (John 11:40).

Cotton Candy. This pleasing fragrance means wrapping things up and transitioning over to operating in the gifts of the Holy Spirit. Sometimes I'll get the smell of cotton candy when preaching, and I know the Lord wants me to begin to conclude my message and step into a time of ministering to the people through the various gifts of the Spirit, such as personal prophecy, praying for the sick, etc. A few years ago, while ministering in South Carolina, I had been preaching in a certain church when the fragrance of cotton candy suddenly manifested strongly in the meeting, and many of us smelled it at the same time. The bishop who was hosting the meeting in his church got a big whiff of it while sitting up on the platform behind the pulpit area. With a puzzled look, he said to me, "What does cotton candy mean?" I said to him, "It means I need to conclude my preaching message and now begin ministering to the people." I quickly concluded my sermon and asked those who needed prayer to come forward. As I slowly went down the line and prayed and laid hands on people, some Christians had visions and heavenly encounters. Some saw angels, others received physical healing, some received deliverance. I think it's important for ministers to always minister God's Word to the people, but we must also be open to the moving of the Spirit and also be willing to go in that direction of ministering to people individually when the Spirit leads.

"Even so you, since you are zealous for spiritual gifts, let it be for the edification of the church that you seek to excel" (1 Corinthians 14:12).

Disinfectant. This scent can often smell like the cleaning products Pine-sol or Lysol. This represents cleansing from evil spirits, and it often comes forth when praying for the sick as they are being healed.

"They shall lay their hands on the sick, and the sick shall recover" (Mark 16:18, Weymouth New Testament).

Evergreen. Always fresh and never outdated, seated with Christ in the high places and being able to see with prophetic eagle-type vision.

"O Ephraim! Stay away from idols! I am living and strong! I look after you and care for you. I am like an evergreen tree, yielding my fruit to you throughout the year" (Hosea 14:8, TLB).

"For he raised us from the dead along with Christ and seated us with him in the heavenly realms because we are united with Christ Jesus" (Ephesians 2:6, NLT).

Finesse Shampoo. A classic shampoo fragrance that represents the anointing and its effect upon your head (your mind), allowing you to smoothly flow in the gifts of the Holy Spirit and move in miracles.

"People were overwhelmed with amazement. 'He has done everything well,' they said. 'He even makes the deaf hear and the mute speak'" (Mark 7:37, NIV).

Frankincense. Frankincense represents that you are receiving a precious gift from God. This is often expressed through being caught in the center of a heavenly portal when you are in a fragrant cloud of frankincense. This signifies that a special prayer request or desire is being granted to you. It means you are going to receive God's very best for your life. The mention of frankincense in the Old Testament was a symbol of faith. In the tabernacle built by Moses, there was the table of showbread in the Holy Place. The twelve loaves of bread on the table represented the twelve tribes of Israel, but the bread was also a prophetic image of Christ, the Word of God in an edible form. The loaves were sprinkled with frankincense and were eaten by the Kohanim (priests) on duty every Sabbath. Your faith in God's word and what He promised to do for you is greatly stirred when the supernatural smell of frankincense appears.

> And you shall take fine flour and bake twelve cakes with it. Two-tenths of an ephah shall be in each cake. You shall set them in two rows, six in a row, on the pure gold table before the Lord. And you shall put pure frankincense on each row, that it may be on the bread for a memorial, an offering made by fire to the Lord.
>
> Leviticus 24:5-7

Fresh-Baked Bread. A fresh message presented through teaching that explains Scripture in a new and living way. This is needed on a regular basis, just like food, in order to maintain spiritual health.

"But He answered and said, 'It is written, "Man shall not live by bread alone, but by every word that proceeds from the mouth of God"'" (Matthew 4:4).

Gardenia. Gardenias have been a favorite wedding flower for generations, so their fragrance can represent getting married or the deep union between Christ and the church.

"Husbands, love your wives, just as Christ also loved the church and gave Himself for her" (Ephesians 5:25).

Grape Juice. Living in the joy of the Lord, staying filled with the Holy Spirit and completely yielded to Him.

> Then he said to them, "Go your way, eat the fat, drink the sweet, and send portions to those for whom nothing is prepared; for this day is holy to our Lord. Do not sorrow, for the joy of the LORD is your strength."
>
> Nehemiah 8:10

Grass. This can be a pleasing smell, but it signifies that there is an attachment to something temporary and passing that is a wrong focus.

"The grass withers, the flower fades, But the word of our God stands forever" (Isaiah 40:8).

Hair Spray. This fragrance usually comes to those who (a) struggle with being intellectually dominant to the neglect of their spirit, (b) think they are always right and never do anything wrong, or (c) are very concerned about their religious dignity. It's God's humorous way of telling those who are in one of these three categories to let their hair down, loosen up, have fun, yield to the Holy Spirit, and be willing to not care about what others think about them.

"I will become even more undignified than this, and I will be humiliated in my own eyes. But by these slave girls you spoke of, I will be held in honor" (2 Samuel 6:22, NIV).

Honey. Revelation from the Word of God, the Scriptures coming alive. It can also represent the flow of revelation knowledge which gives you solutions to the problems and difficulties of life.

"The rules of the LORD are true, and righteous altogether. More to be desired are they than gold, even much fine gold; sweeter also than honey and drippings of the honeycomb" (Psalm 19:9b-10, ESV).

Honeysuckle. This sweet-smelling garden plant speaks of praise. Whenever you smell it, just open your mouth and let your praises go up to the Lord. Angels are present when this fragrance occurs, and they will join with you in praising the Lord.

"But You are holy, enthroned on the praises of Israel" (Psalm 22:3, HCSB).

Horses. This scent can be either positive or negative, depending on the context. Usually, it's positive, and it represents the presence of the angelic army of the Lord. Angels can take the appearance of horses. I have personally seen this multiple times in visions that the Lord has allowed me to have. In my experience, this has always meant that there is a special breakthrough that God wants to do for you and the angels are there to help push it through. This can involve spiritual warfare because the enemy doesn't want you to have a breakthrough. When this happens, it is good to pray, praise, and boldly decree the proclamations that the Holy Spirit will inspire you to make. From a negative perspective, the smell of horses would represent the cravings of the flesh and a love for the impure things of the world.

> The first chariot was pulled by red horses, the second by black horses, the third by white horses, and the fourth by powerful dappled-gray horses. "And what are these, my lord?" I asked the angel who was talking with me. The angel replied, "These are the four spirits of heaven who stand before the Lord of all the earth."
>
> Zechariah 6:2-5a (NLT)

"But he shall not multiply horses for himself, nor cause the people to return to Egypt to multiply horses, for the Lord has said to you, 'You shall not return that way again'" (Deuteronomy 17:16).

Horse Stable (where horses are kept). An invitation to work with angels.

> During the night I had a vision, and there before me was a man mounted on a red horse. He was standing among the myrtle trees in a ravine. Behind him were red, brown and white horses. I asked, "What are these, my lord?" The angel who was talking with me answered, "I will show you what they are." Then the man standing among the myrtle trees explained, "They are the ones the Lord has sent to go throughout the earth."
>
> Zechariah 1:8-10 (NIV)

Ink. The prophetic smell of ink means that you are supposed to write a book. Books are essential in order to impart knowledge and bless humanity. The great preacher Charles Spurgeon had this to say about Apostle Paul, who requested that Timothy bring him books.

> He is inspired, and yet he wants books!
>
> He has been preaching at least for thirty years, and yet he wants books!
>
> He had seen the Lord, and yet he wants books!
>
> He had had a wider experience than most men, and yet he wants books!
>
> He had been caught up into the third heaven, and had heard things which it was unlawful for a men to utter, yet he wants books!
>
> He had written the major part of the New Testament, and yet he wants books!
>
> The apostle says to Timothy and so he says to every preacher, "Give thyself unto reading." The man who never reads will never be read; he who never quotes will never be quoted. He who will not use the thoughts of other men's brains, proves that he has no brains of his own.[7]

"Bring the cloak that I left with Carpus at Troas when you come—and the books, especially the parchments" (2 Timothy 4:13).

Jasmine. Jasmine represents deep spiritual love. It expresses a deeper devotion than what is normally seen among most believers, just as its fragrance is more intense than most other flowers. The distinguishing factor of this deeper love is *thankfulness.*

> And one of them, when he saw that he was healed, returned, and with a loud voice glorified God, and fell down on his face at His feet, giving Him thanks. And he was a Samaritan. So Jesus answered and said, "Were there not ten cleansed? But where are the nine? Were there not any found who returned to give glory to God except this foreigner?"
>
> Luke 17:15-18

Jelly Beans, Black Licorice Scent and Flavor. While jelly beans can come in many different colors and flavors, the licorice smell and taste of the black jelly beans represent healing and praise. Licorice has been used for centuries as a healing medicinal drink. Receive your healing by faith when this smell comes forth and begin to praise the Lord.

"And the prayer of faith will save the one who is sick, and the Lord will raise him up" (James 5:15a, ESV).

Lavender. Lavender means you are washed clean and pure. Its name is derived from a Latin verb that means "to wash" or "to bathe." This name was given to the purple flower because ancient Romans washed their clothes and also took baths with lavender. This became a common practice in Europe for centuries.

"He made the church holy by the power of his word, and he made it pure by washing it with water" (Ephesians 5:26, CEV).

Leather. A new wineskin, a new way of doing things, a new way of thinking.

"And no one puts new wine into old wineskins. If he does, the new wine will burst the skins and it will be spilled, and the skins will be destroyed. But new wine must be put into fresh wineskins" (Luke 5:37-38, ESV).

Lilies. Lilies represent intercessory prayer and self-sacrifice. The "brass sea" used in temple worship was an immense, semicircular vase with ornamental lily work on its edges. It held about 25,000 gallons of water, and its overall appearance was in the shape of a lily. Rabbinic literature says the brass sea represented the nations of the world.[8] We are to pray and make every effort to reach the lost through intercession and by spreading the good news of Jesus Christ to every person on earth. To intercede is to go before the Lord in prayer and entreat Him on behalf of others.

> Then he made the sea of cast metal. It was round, ten cubits from brim to brim, and five cubits high, and a line of thirty cubits measured its circumference. It stood on twelve oxen, three facing north, three facing west, three facing south, and three facing east. The sea was set on them, and all their rear parts were inward. Its

thickness was a handbreadth, and its brim was made like the brim of a cup, like the flower of a lily. It held two thousand baths.

1 Kings 7:23, 25-26 (ESV)

Men's Cologne. Fellowship with your heavenly Father.

"And he will turn the hearts of fathers to their children and the hearts of children to their fathers" (Malachi 4:6a, ESV).

Menthol (same smell as Vicks VapoRub). This minty smell represents the healing of the respiratory system and/or healing from altitude sickness. When you experience this supernatural smell, receive your healing by faith because God's healing power is flowing. Once my daughter became very ill with altitude sickness when we were ministering in the high mountains of Taiwan. We had a doctor check on her, and he recommended that she lay in bed and rest. As she lay there with a fever and aches throughout her body, I laid my hands on her and prayed for her, commanding the sickness to leave in the name of Jesus. I left the room and went straight into a conference meeting where I was scheduled to speak. In my heart, I felt confident that if I took care of the Lord's work, then He would take care of my daughter. When the meeting concluded about two and a half hours later, Kelly and I went directly back to check on Abigail. When we walked into her room, we were amazed to find the entire room engulfed in a supernatural cloud of menthol. Oddly enough, when I asked her about it, she was unaware of the overpowering smell. She made a rapid recovery and was soon back on her feet, enjoying the conference and walking all over the beautiful grounds.

"Let everything that has breath praise the Lord. Praise the Lord" (Psalm 150:6).

Mint. Mint represents healing. When the Holy Spirit is manifesting this fragrance, use your faith to receive the healing you need. If you are physically healthy but still smell this fragrance, then it could represent God's desire to heal your finances. If it's financially related, then use your wallet or purse as a point of contact for prayer;

lay your hands on them or perhaps on your checkbook and command your financial situation to be healed in the name of Jesus.

"And these signs will follow those who believe: In My name they will lay hands on the sick, and they will recover" (Mark 16:17a, 18b).

Mouthwash. Speaking forth a pure and clean word that builds up others.

"You are already clean because of the word which I have spoken to you" (John 15:3).

Musk. The availability of God's power to create or conceive. The gifts of special faith and working of miracles are active when this fragrance is manifesting. When you smell musk, then step out in bold faith and go for it. Natural musk comes from the male muskox and musk deer and is used to attract the females during mating season, which is why the smell is prophetically associated with God's creative power to conceive or birth a miracle.

"By faith Sarah herself also received strength to conceive seed" (Hebrews 11:11).

Myrrh. Myrrh represents physical and emotional healing. The emphasis is strongest on emotional healing because of the way the oil is extracted from the tree. The tree is wounded by stabbing it with a sharp knife, causing the resin to flow out. Emotional wounds are often inflicted through the stabbing effect of cruel words spoken with an intent to hurt the hearer. Harsh words can be extremely destructive, even moving some people to collapse in tears of grief and despair. The hardened resin droplets from the myrrh tree are called "tears," which are harvested by the "tear collector" who takes them to the market where they are sold.

"You keep track of all my sorrows. You have collected all my tears in your bottle. You have recorded each one in your book" (Psalm 56:8, NLT).

Nail polish remover. The wiping away of any sense of shame or inner turmoil caused by false allegations and lies spoken against you.

"Deliver my soul, O Lord, from lying lips And from a deceitful tongue" (Psalm 120:2).

Olives and Olive Oil. The smell of olives or olive oil represents peace and a true anointing.

"Then the dove came to him in the evening, and behold, a freshly plucked olive leaf was in her mouth; and Noah knew that the waters had receded from the earth" (Genesis 8:11).

"Then Samuel took the horn of oil and anointed him in the midst of his brothers. And the Spirit of the LORD rushed upon David from that day forward" (1 Samuel 16:13, ESV).

Onions. Financial provision, money is on the way, enjoying nice things that Egypt (figuratively the world) offers. Once I was visiting the home of the world-renown prophet Bob Jones and his wife Bonnie. Bob had a vision in which he saw both of us walking on a long country road. He told me that we had to keep on walking for four more miles before we reached a large pot with stew in it, with lots of onions. He explained that the onions represented financial provision. I left his home thinking that the interpretation of the vision he saw meant that the four miles were a representation of four days, therefore, I was very excited and expected to see a breakthrough quickly. But it wasn't until four years later that I reached the pot! But it was worth the wait, and I'm glad I kept moving forward. Never give up on your dreams, stay in faith, and God will bring it to pass.

"We remember the fish which we ate freely in Egypt, the cucumbers, the melons, the leeks, the onions, and the garlic" (Numbers 11:5).

Oranges. A zest for life and the energy to actively pursue and accomplish your God-given assignment.

> For it is [not your strength, but it is] God who is effectively at work in you, both to will and to work [that is, strengthening, energizing, and creating in you the longing and the ability to fulfill your purpose] for His good pleasure.
>
> Philippians 2:13 (AMP); brackets in the original

Peppermint. Peppermint speaks of refreshing. This fragrance will, at times, manifest when you discover the truth of what is really going on. The world system is full of lies, false narratives, and fake news. Sometimes this lying spirit can even creep into churches and influence Christians to go along with an evil agenda. How refreshing it is when the veil of deception is pulled back, and you know the truth and walk in the light of it.

"I will refresh the weary and satisfy the faint" (Jeremiah 31:25, NIV).

Pina Colada, Tropical Fragrance. God has a vacation planned for you, somewhere that is warm. Often this refers to a cruise. This can also speak of refreshing and encouragement in cold winter months when God is able to make you happy regardless of the cold climate you may live in or the inclement weather.

My beloved spoke, and said to me:

"Rise up, my love, my fair one,

And come away.

For lo, the winter is past,

The rain is over and gone."

Song of Solomon 2:10-11

Pomegranate. The sweet, tasty, and explosive revelations from God's rhema word. This fruit is eaten throughout Israel, and its many seeds are said to symbolize the commandments of God. It is also the modern-day Hebrew word for "hand grenade" because a pomegranate and hand grenade are both similar in size and weight.

For the Lord your God is bringing you into a good land, a land of brooks of water, of fountains and springs, that flow out of valleys and hills; a land of wheat and barley, of vines and fig trees and pomegranates, a land of olive oil and honey.

Deuteronomy 8:7-8

Poop. Similar to false prophecy and false teaching, this offensive smell is much like the skunk smell. Be on the alert and guard your heart and mind against deception when you smell it.

"Beloved, do not believe every spirit, but test the spirits, whether they are of God; because many false prophets have gone out into the world" (1 John 4:1).

Popcorn. Get ready: good things are going to start happening now. It will be quick and fast. Your harvest is here!

"Don't you have a saying, 'It's still four months until harvest'? I tell you, open your eyes and look at the fields! They are ripe for harvest" (John 4:35, NIV).

Roses. Enduring love relationship with Jesus. This is the most common supernatural fragrance that takes place, and its meaning seems to be instantly understood anywhere in the world.

"I am the rose of Sharon, And the lily of the valleys" (Song of Solomon 2:1).

Saltwater. Positive meaning: called to minister to the nations, international travel.

Negative meaning: anxious, troubled, perhaps angry, and needing to calm down.

"Then the angel said to me, 'The waters you saw, where the prostitute sits, are peoples, multitudes, nations and languages" (Revelation 17:15, NIV).

"You quieted the raging oceans with their pounding waves and silenced the shouting of the nations" (Psalm 65:7, NLT).

Sandalwood. Faithfulness, reverence, and respect toward God, His ministers, and His work. The aloe plant mentioned in the Bible is referring to the fragrant wood called sandalwood, sometimes called agarwood, which produces an oil known as *oud* or aloeswood. What we know in America or the western world as aloe vera is not the same as the aloes mentioned in the Bible. Aloeswood (sandalwood) is very expensive and shows the great wealth of Nicodemus. He brought about a hundred pounds of a mixture of myrrh and aloes, which in today's currency would be over $200,000. The oil extracted from the sandalwood trees has been used for thousands of years, dating back to the pharaohs of Egypt.

After this, Joseph of Arimathea, being a disciple of Jesus, but secretly, for fear of the Jews, asked Pilate that he might take away the body of Jesus; and Pilate gave him permission. So he came and took the body of Jesus. And Nicodemus, who at first came to Jesus by night, also came, bringing a mixture of myrrh and *aloes*, about a hundred pounds.

John 19:38-39

Skunk. False prophet and false prophecy. A false prophet often has signs and wonders that will manifest through occult power. However, their true identity cannot be hidden in the spirit realm. Their repugnant smell reveals who they really are despite their wonderful words and the deceptive miracles they do.

"For false christs and false prophets will rise and show great signs and wonders to deceive, if possible, even the elect" (Matthew 24:24).

Smoke. A level of prayer where you have moved past the outer court, and you are now in the Holy Place where the altar of incense was located. Keep praying and go boldly into the Holy of Holies, where you come before the throne of grace and obtain what you need.

And when he had taken it, the four living creatures and the twenty-four elders fell down before the Lamb. Each one had a harp and they were holding golden bowls full of incense, which are the prayers of God's people.

Revelation 5:8 (NIV)

Steak. A mature word, advanced teaching for believers who are strong in the faith.

"But strong meat belongeth to them that are of full age, even those who by reason of use have their senses exercised to discern both good and evil" (Hebrews 5:14, KJV).

Stock Flower. Longevity and a happy and contented life that is linked to working a job that you love. Work brings dignity, and a good job is a gift from God.

You yourselves know that these hands ministered to my necessities and to those who were with me. In all things I have shown you that by working hard in this way we must help the weak and remember the words of the Lord Jesus, how he himself said, "It is more blessed to give than to receive."

Acts 20:34-35 (ESV)

Strawberries. Friendship with God that comes from having learned the principles of faith in God's unfailing word. It also speaks of good times together.

"And so it happened just as the Scriptures say: 'Abraham believed God, and God counted him as righteous because of his faith.' He was even called the friend of God" (James 2:23, NLT).

Sulfur. A demonic presence. Sometimes (but not always), this smell will manifest when a person is being delivered from demons.

"And the devil, who deceived them, was thrown into the lake of burning sulfur, where the beast and the false prophet had been thrown. They will be tormented day and night for ever and ever" (Revelation 20:10, NIV).

Suntan Lotion. This pleasing smell represents the smooth anointing, a job well done, and resting in the Spirit. This fragrance recently manifested to Kelly and me just after the completion of having a new heating and air-conditioning system installed in our home. It was a two-day extensive work process that went without any problems from start to finish. Everything was done on time, on budget and the finished product exceeded our expectations. As soon as the work was completed and the work crew drove away, the supernatural fragrance of suntan lotion began to swirl around Kelly and me as we stood outside and talked. This was a spiritual indicator of how smooth and well-oiled everything was done on this work project.

"Now all the work of Solomon was well-ordered from the day of the foundation of the house of the Lord until it was finished. So the house of the Lord was completed" (2 Chronicles 8:16).

Tobacco. Tobacco speaks of intimate times of fellowship with the heavenly Father. Of course, we as believers in Christ understand that smelling this pleasing fragrance is not an endorsement for smoking tobacco products which is very harmful. I believe God is still waiting for mankind to discover the proper use of this plant. Since 1746 farmers have known that the tobacco plant is a natural insecticide that can defend other plants from insects. Ranchers have used tobacco leaves for centuries to treat livestock that suffer from bloating and dysentery. Jean Nicot was a French nobleman, scholar, and ambassador to Portugal in the sixteenth century. It was said that while in Portugal, he decided to experiment with tobacco leaves after his chef cut his thumb with a kitchen knife. Nicot wrapped the cut with fresh tobacco leaves and was delighted when the wound completely healed. This intrigued him to experiment further, with claims that Nicot applied tobacco leaves to a young lady's severe facial rash, another to a man who was experiencing sharp pains in his foot, and he placed a tobacco paste on a man's facial tumor, eventually healing all three of their afflictions. When he returned to France, he introduced the plant to the French royal court. It was said to have cured the queen's constant headaches, and its popularity began to expand throughout Europe. His legacy was cemented in the eighteenth century when Swedish botanist Carl Linnaeus named the tobacco plant *Nicotiana* in acknowledgment of Jean Nicot's efforts in promoting the plant's medicinal use.

> In the middle of its street, and on either side of the river, was the tree of life, which bore twelve fruits, each tree yielding its fruit every month. The leaves of the tree were for the healing of the nations.
>
> Revelation 22:2

Vanilla. Vanilla signifies you are in the perfect will of God. Everything is peaceful, and you are in the right place and walking in your purpose intended by the Lord.

"And do not be conformed to this world, but be transformed by the renewing of your mind, that you may prove what is that good and acceptable and perfect will of God" (Romans 12:2).

Violets. Purple violets represent the royalty of the believer in Christ.

"They put a purple robe on him, then twisted together a crown of thorns and set it on him" (Mark 15:17, NIV).

Vinegar. Victory over sin and temptation, successful completion of a divine assignment.

> Later, knowing that everything had now been finished, and so that Scripture would be fulfilled, Jesus said, "I am thirsty." A jar of wine vinegar was there, so they soaked a sponge in it, put the sponge on a stalk of the hyssop plant, and lifted it to Jesus' lips. When he had received the drink, Jesus said, "It is finished." With that, he bowed his head and gave up his spirit.
>
> John 19:28-30 (NIV)

Wet Dog. This smell is revealing to you a homosexual spirit. When I first smelled this, it moved me with great compassion for those who are caught in the snare of homosexuality or lesbianism. The Lord has the power to save, deliver and cleanse all who come to Him.

> And don't forget Sodom and Gomorrah and their neighboring towns, which were filled with immorality and every kind of sexual perversion. Those cities were destroyed by fire and serve as a warning of the eternal fire of God's judgment.
>
> Jude 1:7 (NLT)

Women's Perfume. Positive meaning: a fresh and lovely perfume indicates your position of being seated with Christ in heavenly places (Ephesians 2:6).

Negative Meaning: if it is an unattractive and stale perfume, then it reveals a dry religious spirit. A religious spirit influences believers to move away from a healthy and close relationship with God that is based on salvation by grace, through faith. Instead, it centers on trying to please God through works and tradition. It is only concerned with external righteousness and refuses to accept the new move of the Holy Spirit. It is often critical of those who accept the new.

"But some sneered and said, 'They're full of new wine'" (Acts 2:13, HCSB).

Saints and Scents

For hundreds of years throughout church history, those exceptional saints who lived lives that were sacrificial, morally pure, and virtuous in character were often noted for what was described as having an "odor of sanctity." This odor is a heavenly fragrance that rested upon them and exuded from them as they went about their daily activities during their lifetime. But even after death, many of their bodies continue to emanate a sweet perfume. Because their lives were so devoted to the Lord, His holy qualities were reflected in unique and similar ways, even in death.

"For You will not leave my soul in Sheol, Nor will You allow Your Holy One to see corruption" (Psalm 16:10).

The absence of any smell of corruption upon the bodies of holy saints and the accompanying presence of supernatural perfume being given off has baffled many people. There are many sacred mysteries in the kingdom of God. If we understood all of them, then they would no longer be mysteries. But there are some things about God and His glorious kingdom that we will never fully comprehend, nor are we required to do so. God bears witness to the integrity of His word with signs and wonders, with various miracles (Hebrews 2:4). The very essence of a "wonder" is something beyond our normal experience, which causes us to pause in awe and sincerely question its eternal meaning. The following examples of supernatural fragrance are only a few from the countless signs, wonders, and miracles that God has performed through the regal history of the church.

Bragadino, governor of Cyprus, was a saint, but, like other Cypriots, was a Roman Catholic and maintained at great odds a heroic resistance against the Turks, under the command of Mustapha. When resistance was no longer possible, he surrendered to Mustapha the keys of the city, and was received with well-dissembled courtesy. A cause of complaint was soon invented, and Bragadino being seized was brutally flayed alive. His head, being cut off, was hung to the bowsprit of the admiral's galley, a spectacle of mockery to Turkish soldiers. Pietro Justiniani, an eye witness, asserts that the head for three nights was "englorified with rays like those of the sun, and diffused a most marvelous fragrance."[9]

Saint Hermann (AD 1150–1241) exhaled sweet perfumes from his body.

Every time Saint Hermann of Steinfeld said grace at table, when he was sacristan, he exhaled [...] [the most ravishing odors]. His humility was so great he never knew that the odors proceeded from himself, but used to say each brother of the community smelled sweet with the odors of sanctity.[10]

St. Blandina told St. Clare, who in AD 660 was abbot of Ferriot, that

within three days she and St. Marcel would come to carry his soul into paradise. St. Clare ordered prayer to be made without ceasing both day and night for him; and on the third day, as the choir was chanting the last words of the last psalm—"Let everything that hath breath praise the Lord. Praise ye the Lord"—he gave up the ghost. The chamber was instantly filled with a celestial light, and a fragrance of marvelous sweetness. The buried was buried in St. Blandina's church before the high altar, and the odour which pervaded the chamber at the death of the saint continued with the body till its interment.

St. Hubert died on May 24 [AD 714]; and, when he gave up the ghost, there was diffused over all Brittany an odour so sweet, that it seemed as if God had combined all the perfumes of all the sweet-scented flowers of spring, to symbolize the sanctity of His servant whom He had taken up to paradise.[11]

As [St.] Polycarp entered the arena, a voice from heaven said to him, "Be strong, Polycarp, and play the man," and many of the brethren heard it. On his appearance, the spectators broke into loud clamours. The proconsul exhorted him to purchase liberty by renouncing his faith; but he replied, "Fourscore and six years have I served Christ; how, then, can I now blaspheme my King and Savior?" The fire was then kindled. In compliance with his own request, the aged martyr was not fastened to the stake with iron cramps, but was tied with cords. The flames, instead of touching him, swept round his body, "like the sails of a ship filled with wind," and the hoary saint appeared in the midst of this fiery tent, like gold glowing in a furnace; and a perfume sweeter than frankincense issued from him, filling the whole air. One of the executioners, to hasten his death, stabbed him with a sword, and the blood from the wound put out the fire.[12]

When Onulf was sent to fetch away the dead body of St. Severin, that had been buried six years, it was not only undecayed, but it gave out a most exceedingly sweet fragrance, "though no embalmer's hand had ever touched it."

St. Valery from his sanctity, even in life, exhaled a sweet odour (AD 619). One day St. Colomban was explaining to his monks the subject of a lecture, when all of a sudden the room was filled with a celestial odour. The abbot asked who it was that had just entered, and being told it was Brother Valery, he cried in transport, "O my beloved, it is you, not I, who are the veritable head of this monastery."

As soon as St. Xavier [1506–1552] was dead, his body was laid in a coffin filled with pure lime to consume the flesh. Four months afterwards, when the coffin was opened, it was found that the grave-clothes were wholly uninjured, and the flesh was as fresh as if the body had but just died. No sort of effluvia was perceptible, but, on the contrary, an agreeable odour. Putting the body back with more lime, the coffin was taken to Malacca, which at the time was troubled with plague; but the moment the coffin arrived, the plague ceased. A new coffin was made, but it was too small, and as the dead body was forced down, blood issued from the shoulders, and stained the shroud. The coffin was buried in the churchyard of Our Blessed Lady, and in nine months was again opened, when the body was still fresh, and the blood on the napkin moist. The body was now laid in a most sumptuous coffin, and carried to the Indies. It was received at Goa with great pomp, the viceroy himself taking part in the ceremony. No ointment, spices, or balm had been used; but the body "had a ravishing fragrance," and was laid on the right side of the high altar.[13]

Saint Thérèse of Lisieux (1873–1897)

Thérèse was a French Carmelite nun. The world came to know her through her autobiography, *Story of a Soul,* which was released after her death. In her writings, she said, "What matters in life is not great deeds, but great love." She determined to do the simple things in life well and to do them with extraordinary love. Thérèse loved flowers, especially roses, and saw herself as the "little flower of Jesus" who gave glory to God by just being herself among all the other flowers in God's garden. She said,

> Every flower created by Him [God] is beautiful, that the brilliance of the rose and the whiteness of the lily do not lessen the perfume of the violet or the sweet simplicity of the daisy. [...] If all the lowly flowers wished to be roses, nature would lose its springtide beauty, and the fields would no longer be enameled with lovely hues. And so it is in the world of souls, our Lord's living garden.[14]

Because of this fitting analogy, the title "The Little Flower of Jesus" has come to remain with St. Thérèse. In the final month, before she passed away from a lung disease at the age of twenty-four, she promised, "When I die, I will send down a shower of roses from the heavens, I will spend my heaven by doing good on earth." Her last words just before dying were, "My God, I love you!" Upon her death, the convent was filled with the heavenly fragrance of roses, which remained for days. She is buried in Lisieux, France, where over two million visitors come each year to show their love and appreciation for her.

Kathryn Kuhlman (May 9, 1907–February 20, 1976). Image courtesy of Toronto Star Photograph Archive, courtesy of Toronto Public Library

Time magazine said, "She is, in fact, a veritable one-woman shrine of Lourdes."[15] She displayed one of the strongest healing anointings that the church has ever seen.

Kathryn Kuhlman was known for her deep relationship with the Holy Spirit.

She developed such a close relationship with the Holy Spirit that Dr. Oral Roberts [who saw her ministering] said, "It was like they were talking backwards and forth to each other, and you couldn't tell where Kathryn started and the Holy Spirit left off. It was a oneness."[16]

Her ministry demonstrated God's supernatural ability to heal the sick, causing a diverse multitude of people to come from all over the world to experience the awesome presence and power of God in her meetings.

Later in life, when she became ill and was very weak and on a respirator, Kathryn was attended by a young nurse who covered the night shift at the CCU (Coronary Care Unit) at the hospital. Although Kathryn Kuhlman passed away in 1976, this Christian nurse shared about the events surrounding her passing in 2020. Kathryn had been admitted at Hillcrest Hospital in Tulsa, Oklahoma. The hospital at that time had 800 beds, and because of its large size, one of the hospital units was on the other side of a four-lane road. Shortly after 1 o'clock in the morning, the nurse was alerted by the monitor that showed Kathryn's heartbeat rhythm had straight-lined (which is an indication of death). At that exact moment, the electrical power in the entire hospital went out. The nurse entered Kathryn's room and checked for a heartbeat, but there was none. The nurse stepped out of the room and contacted her supervisor, telling her that Kathryn had just passed. The supervising nurse said she would come right over, noting it would take her a few minutes to get there. (The supervisor had to go down three flights of stairs, then walk through a tunnel beneath the four-lane road and come back up again on the other side.) Meanwhile, the nurse stepped back into Kathryn's room, and when she did, she noticed what she later described as, "The absolute warmest, thickest, most overwhelming smell of roses absolutely flooded the room."[17] She continued by saying, "It was so hot and so thick I had trouble staying in the room and breathing." The nurse stepped out into the hallway to breathe. Soon the supervising nurse arrived, and her first remark was, "Well, this is where that smell is coming from!" She was able to smell it at the other extension of the hospital that was across the four-lane road. As she walked through the tunnel, the smell had gotten stronger and stronger. The nurse on duty pointed to Kathryn's room and sweetly said, "That is where the smell is coming from." The supervisor said, "Well, you guys aren't allowed to have roses in here." The nurse responded by saying, "We don't have any flowers in here." Kathryn had told the nurses on the day shift a few days earlier that the only flower she wanted at her funeral was roses.

The whole story of Kathryn Kuhlman's life was one of miracles. The words of the psalmist are especially comforting at the passing of God's mighty servants who poured out their lives to bless the Lord's people and to reach lost souls.

"Precious in the sight of the LORD is the death of His saints" (Psalm 116:15).

Corrie ten Boom (April 15, 1892–April 15, 1983)

The ten Boom family, led by Corrie's father, hid Jews in a well-concealed hiding place within their home. The Jews were being sought by the Gestapo for arrest and deportation during the German occupation of the Netherlands during World War II. In a Gestapo raid on their home, most of the ten Boom family was captured, but some were later released. However, Corrie and her older sister Betsie and their father were put in prison. The father soon died, and Corrie and Betsie were transferred to various prisons before being sent to the Ravensbruck death camp, where Betsie eventually died. One week before all women prisoners her age were executed, Corrie was released due to a clerical error. After the war was over, she went on to travel the world as an ambassador of forgiveness. She always shared the good news of salvation in Jesus Christ. She is referred to by Jewish leaders as being a "righteous Gentile" because of having risked her life to protect Jews. This acknowledgment is further highlighted by a Jewish understanding that it is considered a special blessing of God to die on the same day you were born, which is what happened to Corrie on April 15. Rabbi Menachem Posner shares further insight into this concept;

> The Chassidic masters explain that on the day we are born we are entrusted with a mission. The righteous person lives his life achieving his fullest potential and completes his mission on earth in the most perfect way possible. This perfection is expressed in the fact that his mission ends on the very same day that it was begun.[18]

Corrie died at the age of ninety-one, which appears to be another favor bestowed by God that carries a Jewish tie-in. Corrie was known for her best-selling book, which was made into a famous movie called *The Hiding Place*, which is based upon Psalm 91. Corrie's life was inseparably linked to the Jewish people. The woman who cared for Corrie ten Boom in her last years perceived a beautiful scent that she said emanated from Corrie's presence, which was, "Something like the scent of orange blossoms."[19] The soft scent of orange blossoms would represent energy and comfort. It was said of Corrie that even in her mid-eighties, there were very few people who could keep up with her because of her energy and hectic schedule. Also, her message was one of soothing comfort, especially to survivors of the Holocaust, who needed loving guidance to forgive those who caused them so much hurt and pain.

Padre Pio showing the stigmata,
taken from a photo dated August 19, 1919

When it comes to saints who exuded the "odor of sanctity" when they were alive, without question, one of the world's most well-known was Padre Pio. He was born in 1887 and passed away in 1968. As a Franciscan priest, he lived in the monastery at San Giovanni Rotondo, Italy. There are three main categories of Franciscans, which are Observants, Conventuals, and Capuchins. All three religious orders follow the rule of Saint Francis, and all endeavor to live the life exemplified by Francis. Padre Pio belonged to the Capuchin order of Franciscans.

Each day he would awaken at 2:30 a.m. to begin his prayers and prepare for the morning mass. Between mass and confessions, his normal work day would sometimes last up to nineteen hours. He was sustained by God's grace through holy communion and lived on only two or three hours of sleep each night. His lifestyle of fasting consisted of eating only 300–400 calories of food per day, an amount insufficient even for a young child to survive on. He never took a day of vacation in his fifty-one years of ministry, nor did he ever listen to the radio or read a newspaper. God anointed him with many mystical favors, including prophecy, the ability to read hearts, the prophetic ability to see angels, and he also carried the stigmata (the sacred wounds of Christ) in his physical body in his hands, feet, and side. From these wounds and from his body would issue forth the most amazing fragrances, including smells of violets, lilies, roses, the sweet aroma of fresh tobacco, and other beautiful heavenly scents. Even though he passed away decades ago, over eight million pilgrims visit his grave site each year.

In the year 2000, there was a Christian woman who greatly enjoyed my ministry. She was the head librarian over a very large library in a metropolitan city in southern California. One day she gave me a book from the library about the life of Padre Pio. She kindly insisted I read it, stating that she felt it was necessary for me to know about his life. This woman wasn't Catholic; she was a Pentecostal Christian. At the moment, it seemed to me to be kind of humorous for an evangelical Pentecostal woman to be so adamant that I read a book about a Catholic priest from Italy who I had never heard of before. However, by the time I had finished reading through the first chapter, I was hooked. Soon, after reading the entire book in just a few days, I returned it to her, and then she gave me another book about him, written by a different author. Moving beyond the library in my research and spiritual hunger to know more about those who had a deep walk with God, I soon purchased more books on the life of Padre Pio and devoured them all, some of them being rather large in content with around 400 pages.

Faith comes by hearing. We are instructed to hear the Word of God. The more we hear it, the stronger our faith becomes. Hearing and meditating upon the story of Padre Pio was one method that the Holy Spirit used to begin to bring forth into my life and ministry very similar and even unique manifestations concerning supernatural fragrances. This knowledge also led me down the "ancient path of the saints," where I studied and discovered many holy men and women who lived like Enoch while on the earth, with the "odor of sanctity" being evidenced in their lives. Over the years, as Kelly and I have traveled around the world ministering the gospel, these heavenly fragrances come forth as a positive sign of the Lord's presence, of prayers being answered, of comfort to those in distress, of divine warning of some type of danger and as a confident assurance that lets you know when to step out in faith and go for it because the Lord is with you.

The Lord is so good. He will always bring into your life exactly what you need for your healthy spiritual diet. The prophetic ministry of Padre Pio has added color to my life and ministry, and I will always be deeply appreciative of my librarian friend, who was open to cross-pollinating and swimming in more than just one stream of Christianity. Just as Israel is one nation, but yet composed of twelve different tribes with their own distinct qualities, so we as the body of Christ are one church, while at the same time we are composed of various "tribes" and expressions of the Christian faith within the church. We see this foreshadowed through Joseph's coat of many colors. It was one coat, but the various colors complemented each other, thus representing the beauty of the collective church.

An entire chapter could be written concerning the many testimonies of those who encountered supernatural fragrance in connection with the humble and beloved Franciscan priest, Padre Pio. Here are a few for you to enjoy.

Friar Modestino said: "Once I was on vacation at St. Giovanni Rotondo. I went to Padre Pio in the sacristy that morning to serve the Holy Mass, but other monks were already arguing in the sacristy as to who would have this privilege. Padre Pio interrupted those discussions by saying—'only he will serve the Holy Mass'—and he pointed me out! I accompanied Padre Pio to St. Francis altar, I closed the gate, and I started to serve the Holy Mass in profound awe. When the Mass got to the point of the 'Sanctus' I suddenly had a desire to smell again that indescribable perfume that I had already perceived when I had kissed Padre Pio's hand. The desire was immediately granted me and it was like I was wooed by St. Pio's perfume. The perfume increased more and more, so much so that the perfume caused me to breathe irregularly. I leaned my hand on the communion rail so as not to fall! I was about to faint when I mentally asked Padre Pio to save me from embarrassment in front of the people. In that precise instant the perfume disappeared. In the evening, while I accompanied him to his room, I asked Padre Pio for an explanation about that phenomenon. He answered me: 'My child, I am not able to explain it. God intervenes to allow somebody to smell the perfume whenever He wants.'"[20]

Bishop Raffaello Carlo Rossi was sent by the pope in 1921 to carry out a thorough investigation regarding all the miraculous reports and rumors surrounding Padre Pio. This investigation was not carried out due to suspicion but rather to gather an unbiased report of what the actual facts were concerning the supernatural phenomena surrounding his life. Bishop Rossi had this to say concerning his careful observations:

> This very intense and pleasant fragrance, similar to the scent of the violet—as it was well described by the Bishop of Melfi—is attested by everyone, and may the Most Eminent Fathers let me attest it, too. I have smelled it, just as I have seen the 'stigmata.' And I can again assure the Most Eminent Fathers that I went to San Giovanni Rotundo with the resolute intention of conducting an absolutely objective inquiry, but also with a real personal unfavorable prejudice regarding what was said about Padre Pio. Today I am not a...convert, and admirer of the Padre: certainly not; I feel complete indifference and I would say almost coldness, so much did I want to maintain a serene objectivity in writing my report. But, to clear my conscience, I have to say that, faced with some of the facts, I could not retain my personal unfavorable prejudice, even though I did not manifest anything on the outside. And one of these facts is the fragrance, which, I'll repeat, I have sensed, just like everyone else. The only one who does not notice it is Padre Pio.[21]

Dr. Giorgio Festa was one of the early examiners of Padre Pio's wounds. He was a skilled and highly esteemed surgeon from Rome who was commissioned by the Capuchin general to examine Padre Pio's stigmata. He testified:

> I can affirm that on my first visit I took from his side a small cloth stained with blood which I brought back with me to Rome for a microscopic examination. I personally, being entirely deprived of the sense of smell, did not notice any special emanation. But a distinguished official and other persons with me in the automobile on our return to Rome from San Giovanni, not knowing that I brought with me that piece of cloth enclosed in a case, despite the strong ventilation due to the speed of the automobile, smelled the fragrance very distinctly and assured me that it precisely corresponded to the perfume which emanates from the person of Padre Pio. In Rome, in the succeeding days and for a long time after, the same cloth conserved in a cabinet in my study filled the room with perfume—so much that many patients who came to consult me spontaneously asked me for an explanation of its origin.[22]

A gentleman met Father Pio through a series of strange coincidences. He says: "The first time I heard somebody speak of this extraordinary religious man was after the war. A friend of mine knew the Padre well. He spoke enthusiastically of him. But I thought to myself his stories about the holy man were a bit much. So I must confess my initial reactions were indifference and disbelief. This was especially true when my friend told me about various phenomena attributed to Padre Pio, especially the scent of perfumes. Many people claim to detect an aroma of perfume even when they are not anywhere near the sainted Friar. You can imagine my surprise when this started to happen to me. I would catch the aroma of violets in unusual places, where even the hint of a flower could not be found. I began to wonder about myself. I started to doubt my senses. I even told myself I must be dreaming. One day the phenomenon happened when I was on vacation with my wife. I had gone to the post office to mail a letter. The post office in question did not normally lace its air with perfume. I don't know of any that do. But all of a sudden I smelled the unmistakable odor of violets. Catching the scent, my wife said to me 'Where is this odor of perfume coming from?'

Excitedly, I asked her, 'Can you smell it too?' Then I told my wife about Padre Pio and about the stories of unusual perfumed aromas surrounding his presence. These aromas could be detected even if one were at a distance from the good Padre. My wife was moved. She said to me: 'If I were you, I would leave for San Giovanni Rotondo right away.' The next day, we were on our way. We met with Padre Pio and he said to me, 'Ah, here is our hero. How much effort I expended to get you here.' That same day, I had a chance to speak with Padre Pio personally. From that moment on, my life was changed."[23]

Monk Ludovico of St. Giovanni Rotondo said that "Padre Pio left a wake of perfume, when he passed for the several places of the convent."[24]

Father Fred said, "Sometimes, if you wanted to know where Padre Pio was, it was enough to follow the wake of the perfume."[25]

A lawyer who was very devoted to Father Pio says: "Once I was in the old church in the monastery attending one of Padre Pio's long Masses. At the moment of the consecration of the Sacred Host, I became distracted. I was the only person standing in the middle of the crowd of believers who were all kneeling. Suddenly, I was overwhelmed by a powerful aroma of violets. The scent was so strong it jolted me back to the present moment. Looking around me, I knelt down without thinking anything about the unusual perfume that hovered above me. As was my custom, after the Mass was over, I went to greet Padre Pio. He welcomed me saying 'Were you a little disoriented today?' I sheepishly said 'Yes, Padre. I have been a bit absent-minded today, but fortunately, your perfume woke me up.' He said simply: 'For you, perfume is not necessary. For you, slaps are necessary.'"[26]

Saint Benedict (AD 480–547) may have lived 1,500 years ago, but he wrote a very famous book that went on to become one of the most influential works in all of western Christendom. His book, *The Rule*, was a set of instructions for how a monk was to conduct his life in a monastery. St. Benedict founded monasteries and was greatly used by

God as an evangelist among the pagans. He had a famous sister who was a nun; she also had a deep walk with God, her name was Saint Scholastica. Benedict was known for the many miracles that occurred in his ministry, such as making an iron ax head that had fallen into the lake float, the miraculous multiplication of oil during a famine, causing a stone to be lifted that workers constructing a monastery could not move because the devil was sitting on it, prophesying the future accurately to many people including a startling prophecy to King Totila, king of the Goths in which he told Totila to repent of his sins, for within ten years he would be dead, which occurred exactly as was spoken.

Biographer and Roman statesman Cassiodorus, who knew Benedict and was highly influenced by him, tells us the following:

His tunic—and he had but one—just like his skin, gives forth a sweeter fragrance than all the perfumes of India, thus proving that the human body can have its own good odor, provided it be not defiled with overindulgence in eating or drinking, by reason of which it gives forth a stench. It can easily be seen that divine Omnipotence deigns to visit such a man, when we ourselves are delighted by his presence...After treating at length of the soul, we have also put down with regard to the human body what we have seen.[27]

St. Paul of the Cross had many visions
and supernatural encounters with the Lord

Saint Paul of the Cross (1694–1775), originally named Paolo Francesco Daneii, is considered by many church historians to be the greatest Christian mystic of the eighteenth century. He is most known for having founded the Passionists order within the Roman Catholic Church, which is an order that is devoted to contemplating the sufferings that Jesus endured for us through His trial and crucifixion. Like all of the saints, he was richly blessed with spiritual gifts, and the highest expressions of love, giving, and self-sacrifice were consistently displayed throughout his life. He also emitted a scent from his body that was not from this world, as we see from the following testimonies.

> Our Lord, as if He wished to manifest, by unusual and miraculous signs, the servant of God's purity, ordained that, more than once, several persons should perceive a perfume and most fragrant sweetness, not to be compared to any ordinary scent, either in kissing his hand, in approaching him, in taking hold of his handkerchief, wet with perspiration after he had been preaching, or of any sign of the Passion which he had worn, or in entering the rooms inhabited by him, as is attested in the Processes. At Aspra, in Sabina, Doctor Felix Bruschi, having received the good Father in his house, perceived, as soon as he departed, in the room which he had inhabited, a singular fragrance, and considering it something extraordinary and wonderful, he called his family, saying with amazement and a deep feeling of devotion, "Smell, smell what a perfume! What a fragrance! Oh, what a fragrance!" The same thing occurred at Fianello, when Signora Juliana Angelini and Antonia Pacelli, on entering the room Father Paul had occupied during the mission, immediately smelt a sweet perfume, unlike anything they had ever before experienced; and what is more, this scent, like something supernatural, caused in them a special devotion, by which they were more than ever confirmed in the opinion they entertained of the holiness and spotless purity of the servant of God.

The same wonderful fragrance was noticed in other rooms occupied by him; and one who for a considerable time had the consolation of being near him attests that, besides the fragrance emitted from his body and his habit "which I myself (these are the witness's words) have perceived by remaining with him, especially in the Retreat of the Presentation at Orbetello, and that at Toscanella, when I served him as secretary and was obliged to be near him, the same fragrance was perceptible in the cell where he slept." The same is attested by another religious, who, without being told of it by anyone, which might have caused it to be considered imagination or prejudice, more than once perceived an unusual perfume in Father Paul's room; and once, when the servant of God left the Retreat at Cerra, the sweet perfume of the room he had occupied was perceptible for six months; and the religious, having mentioned this fact to the Father Superior, was told by him that he had noticed the same thing. Thus, our Lord more and more manifested the purity of His servant and made it an object of veneration. Paul, who knew very well how precious is this great treasure, renounced constantly and generously, in order to preserve and possess it, all the allurements and the great hopes that the world offered him, and among them an honorable and advantageous marriage, as we have said.[28]

He also could detect the sin in others by a foul odor.

He could smell such a stench from the bodies of persons guilty of impurity that he could not endure it and almost fainted. In fact, he did so once when someone guilty of many of these sins went to his confessional. Another time a young man asked to be admitted to St. Paul's order. The saint knew nothing of the young man's character but took both the young man's hands in his and remarked, "You know how much you have offended God with these hands, and you would say Mass!"[29]

When you study the lives of saints within the church, you realize that there are genuine proofs that testify to the validity of a life that is pleasing to the Lord. Anytime there is a genuine heavenly gift, the devil will always present a counterfeit. This is true when it comes to supernatural fragrances. Without mentioning names of certain unsaved men that could possibly draw needless attention to them, I can say I am very familiar with those in other religions who can bring forth miracle fragrances through the empowerment of deceiving spirits who possess them. This is not surprising because the devil can operate under the false premises of being an angel of light in an attempt to deceive. However, the apostle Paul said that anyone who preachers "another gospel" should be accursed. There are many false religions and spirits of deception that are on the earth. But one thing is for sure: you may be able to manifest different fragrances through evil spirits, but you can't fake moral purity and obedience to the commandments of God. You either keep the Scriptures, or you break them. Obedience to God's commandments and a life of holiness are hallmarks of the mature saint. The devil is a law-breaker; he is constantly tempting people to get in the flesh and sin. The Holy Spirit empowers us to walk in victory over the world, the flesh, the devil, and every temptation the enemy may bring.

As believers, righteousness is a position that we receive because of our identity in Christ. Righteousness is based upon what Jesus did for us through His death, burial, and resurrection. Righteousness is an attribute of God that is imparted to the believer. But holiness is vastly different. Holiness is developed in the life of the individual believer. Through the blessing of spiritual inheritance and covenant birthright, you are now positioned in Him, and you are declared righteous.

"God made him who had no sin to be sin for us, so that in him we might become the righteousness of God" (2 Corinthians 5:21, NIV).

Holiness is separation from the world, the flesh, and the devil. Holiness takes place when you are joined to God, who alone is holy. There is a difference between holiness and innocence in that holiness contains real-life experiences of being tried and tested. When we resist temptation and make the right choices, we promote holiness in our lives. Righteousness is granted simply because of your faith in God and your born-again position in Him; it is given to you from God as a gift undeserved. We have been saved by grace through faith, and we can't take credit for this; it is a gift from God. It is very much possible to be righteous but not be holy. One of the clearest biblical examples of a man who demonstrated the difference between righteousness and holiness was Lot. Apostle Peter reminds us that Lot lived in Sodom and that the behavior of the Sodomites brought much anguish to his soul.

> Lot, who was oppressed by the filthy conduct of the wicked (for that righteous man, dwelling among them, tormented his righteous soul from day to day by seeing and hearing their lawless deeds).
>
> 2 Peter 2:7-8

Notice how God describes the conduct of homosexuality as *filthy conduct*. The world may applaud this lifestyle and present it as being acceptable, but it grieves the heart of God because it is a perversion of a person's nature who is made in the image of God. Forgiveness and full deliverance can be found for anyone trapped in homosexuality. Jesus came to set us free from every type of bondage to sin. This is the day and hour for full redemption for all who come to Jesus for deliverance and protective shelter.

Lot didn't approve of these sins, but nevertheless, he willingly chose to place himself and his family right in the middle of a dark spiritual stronghold. Lot was governed by his eyes and his natural senses. Because Abraham and Lot had much livestock, Abraham said they needed to separate. Abraham invited Lot to choose the land that he wanted, and Abraham promised that he would go in another direction. Lot chose to live in the cities of the plain, in Sodom. He did this even though he knew that "the men of Sodom were exceedingly wicked and sinful against the Lord" (Genesis 13:13). Before God destroyed the city, he sent two angels to deliver Lot and his family. With great difficulty, the angels got Lot, his wife, and two daughters out of the city, literally having to grab them by their hands and pull them out of their house. In the process of fleeing, Lot's wife disregarded the angels' instruction and looked back, and became a pillar of salt.

From the biblical record, we see that Lot was righteous but not holy. A holy person would never choose to live in a place, regardless of how beautiful it was, if it placed unrelenting pressure upon themself and their family to participate in iniquity. Sin stinks! Sin is a reproach to nations and individuals. Make a clean and determined break from the practice of sin today. We must allow the Lord to work in our hearts where we are desirous to progress from righteousness to holiness.

"Righteousness exalts a nation, But sin is a reproach to any people" (Proverbs 14:34).

There is a man in church history known as the Flying Monk. That statement may stretch some who are not familiar with the miracle-working power of God, but God's wonder-working ability is still displayed through His people today. The more time you spend in God's house (not the bar, nightclub, or lecture hall of the atheist), the more you realize that God has performed literally millions of miracles throughout the church age and that miracles still occur every single day around the world. I have different books in my personal library listing numerous saints who were regularly lifted up into the air by the Holy Spirit. But this is not something hidden under a bushel; this has happened to countless saints around the world. I have a picture on my phone of a Pentecostal minister preaching before a large audience while he is supernaturally suspended several feet above the platform, as he hovers in the air with the crowd watching him while he preaches a powerful message under the anointing of the Holy Spirit with his feet not touching anything. All of this falls under the category of signs, wonders, and miracles.

"God also testified to it by signs, wonders and various miracles, and by gifts of the Holy Spirit distributed according to his will" (Hebrews 2:4, NIV).

Brother Joseph illustrated in one of his many flights

God goes to great lengths to reach the lost with the gospel of salvation by displaying signs, wonders, and different types of miracles. Joseph of Cupertino was given by God as a sign gift to the church to display His grace and power. Whenever Joseph would have one of his many visions, he would simultaneously be lifted up physically by the Holy Spirit. Although the pope wisely tried to keep Joseph hidden away in Italy's most remote monasteries to shield the sacredness of such miracles, the word still got out, and the crowds came, hoping to get a glimpse of him. All it took was someone within the monastery to mention to Joseph a sweet word about Jesus or to speak about a beloved passage of scripture, and up he would go, sometimes staying in the air for as long as forty-five minutes. He was witnessed suspended in the air by royalty, princes and princesses, ambassadors of kings and European nobles from visiting nations, as well as by monks, bishops, cardinals, and even by the pope himself. My favorite story of Joseph was when he came from a Sunday service, having just heard the reading of the Gospel account of Christ as the Good Shepherd. After dinner, Joseph and the monks went to the garden, where Joseph saw one of the monastery's lambs. Upon expressing a desire to hold it, one of the monks placed it in his arms, where Joseph sweetly hugged it. The more love he poured on the little lamb, the more excited he became as the Spirit of the Lord moved on him. He then took the lamb and, with superhuman ease, threw it high into the air, with Joseph then rising up in the air next to it high above the trees. They both stayed up in the air above the trees for over two hours in a kneeling position. He was truly the flying monk. Here is an excerpt regarding the life of Joseph of Cupertino.

As much as Joseph loved purity, he hated the opposing vice, and he smelled the stink of anyone stained with such guilty iniquity. One day he was seen disturbed and restless, and when asked what the matter was, he answered

> that he had just spoken with a woman filthy with sensuality and that she had left such a stink in his nostrils that he couldn't remove it. For that reason, one shouldn't wonder that he frequently repeated to everyone that impure people stink in the divine presence and in the presence of angels and men, whereas chaste people have "Christi bonus odor et odorem notitae suae manifestant in omni loco" (the fragrance of Christ, and of their reputations are evident everywhere).[30]

By virtue of his unsullied purity, Joseph was rewarded by God with the prized gift of fragrance sensed by everyone, which was so pleasing, so continuous in his body, in his clothing, in his cell, and finally in everything he touched. It stupefied anyone who smelled the fragrance and will stupefy in the future anyone who hears this certain and authentic narration:

> Father Joseph of Copertino [so deposes Father Francis Maria de' Angelis, a monk of the Minor Order] sent out and exuded from his body and from his clothing a sweetest odor, which was unlike any natural or artificial odor I have ever smelled. And the same fragrance spread from him throughout his whole room. It was recognized as his, and he left his fragrance wherever he passed by, which I smelled throughout the whole time that I was active in

that holy monastery, and which I have meant to say publicly, and which lasted until his death as a sign of his purity and chastity.[31]

The same was deposed by Father Peter Francis Levanto, Minor Observant and President of the Monastery of the New Church of Assisi, who said:

I know that the room where Father Joseph lived in this holy monastery like the clothing he wore, yielded an odor and fragrance of Heaven, it not being possible for it to be anything natural, and I couldn't determine its nature...When I used to return to the monastery after having gone to Father Joseph's room, the fathers would ask me what I was wearing on my body, and I would tell them truthfully that I was not wearing anything with a fragrance, but the fragrance came from my having gone to the room of Father Joseph, and at times it stayed on me for fifteen days.[32]

Don Girolamo delgi Angelucci added,

As corroboration of Joseph's chastity, God had bestowed a great and most sweet fragrance upon him that covered his body, his clothing, and everything he touched...and anybody could easily find his cell because the fragrance spread even beyond it...I could not tell you what strong natural odor it resembled, but I and others have always valued it as a gift of God.[33]

The same is deposed by Doctor Baldassare Massichi, and the Father-Regent Barnanei, and the Gonfalonier of Assis, Graziano Benigni. And, Father Brother Giovanni Maria Cappuccino of Fossombrone attests that

The fragrance that emanated from the body of Father Guiseppe (Father Joseph) was so abundant and pleasing that it cheered all those who entered his cell, and was spread even outside, a sign to those who might not have known where Father Joseph was that he could be found by the sweetness of the fragrance. That fragrance spread to all the cells where he might be visiting for a short while, in the clothing he wore, which, even though I had them washed many times with lye and soap, never lost their sweet odor.[34]

So it was on the priestly vestments used by him, which not only retained the fragrance but communicated it to the chests where they were kept and then to other vestments, and the same happened with the things that he touched. So everyone concluded that any such odor *was the odor of paradise, the fragrance of paradise.*

To these noble testimonies, we add the deposition of the surgeon, Francis Pier Paoli, who testifies,

> It is most certainly true that, as a sign of Father Joseph's most clear purity and chastity, the Lord God endowed him with a most strong fragrance which always breathed out from his body, and I know it because all the time I attended him, as I said many times before, and handling him and moving him in his final infirmity, I could always smell that fragrance, which one knew full well to be supernatural, there not being any natural odor similar to it.[35]

The image is by Italian painter Ludovico Mazzanti from the 1700s

It didn't take much to cause Joseph to be lifted in flight. Sometimes, just mentioning to him in reverent conversation the name of Jesus or Mary or the Holy Spirit would cause him to fall into a visionary trance, and he would then begin to ascend. He is the patron saint of pilots, astronauts, and those with a learning disability.

Two most eminent ecclesiastics now close this chapter, and the high quality of these people renders even more authentic the truth of the narrative. Julius Cardinal Spinola, who was an admirer of the stupendous raptures of the Blessed One, also participated personally in smelling the so-miraculous fragrance. "When I entered that small cell, I said to him that I felt myself soothed by a most smooth fragrance, a sweetest odor, that I couldn't say what I could compare it to among those of nature or those composed artificially, but it is certain that although all other odorous things annoy me, I felt extraordinary pleasure from that which came from that cell, which even seemed to confer bodily health on me."

One finally hears Joseph's old acquaintance, that is, cardinal di Lauria, a person well known to the world, distinguished for his piety and excelling in doctrine. In his words, "The notable gift of Joseph's purity has been evident to all those who have either dealt with him or had anything touched by him, for it yielded a most sweet odor, and the things handled by him kept the odor for a long time. In fact, in the dormitories through which he would pass, he left such a discernible odor that in order to find out where Brother Joseph had gone it was only necessary to follow the path of the odor. It is certain, as the teachers of the spiritual life tell us, that a person's odor is the sign of true purity and the cleanliness of his heart."[36]

Volumes of pages could be written about the various men and women of God throughout the church's beautiful history who have emitted the fragrance of Christ. Israel was one nation but comprised of twelve distinct tribes. In a similar way, the church is one large family of God, comprised of believers from various streams of the Christian faith. Regardless of where you look, be it in the Protestant church, the Catholic church, Eastern Orthodox church, or some other variant of the Christian faith, you will certainly find those noted individuals whose close walk with God is evidenced through supernatural fragrance. Church history continues to be written. May you develop into mature sainthood and be found among the faithful who glorify God with a life that is lived to bring honor to Him. The end-time church that you are a part of is destined to be a glorious bride without any stain or wrinkle in her garment, holy, and without flaws in character and conduct. Upon the Lord's return, the church will be like a bouquet of flowers, made up of individual flowers (individual believers) that, when placed together (the collective body of Christ), will produce the most beautiful and astonishing fragrance the world has ever known.

What Is a Prophetic Fragrance?

Did you ever stop to consider that fragrance is prophetic? What do I mean when I say something is *prophetic*? To be prophetic means that an object or thing contains the nature and essence of prophecy. What then is prophecy? In its most basic and personal sense, prophecy is an inspired message from God that reveals future insight about your life. Prophecy can be delivered through many different methods. One way in which prophecy can be shared is when it is spoken forth, often by a prophet. There are scriptures in the Old Testament spoken by prophets that unveil future events regarding the Messiah. Isaiah was a prophet who lived seven hundred years before the time of Jesus, yet he gave deep prophetic insight concerning the life, mission, and purpose of Jesus. He described with remarkable detail the agonies that Messiah Jesus would endure at the cross of Calvary, as well as the ultimate accomplishment that He would achieve by taking away sin. The book of Isaiah is the most comprehensive picture of Jesus in the Old Testament. This can be clearly seen as you read slowly through the following verses, keeping in mind that Jesus would not be on the earth until hundreds of years in the future from the actual time when Isaiah gave this prophecy.

See, my servant will act wisely;

he will be raised and lifted up and highly exalted.

Just as there were many who were appalled at him—

his appearance was so disfigured beyond that of any human being

and his form marred beyond human likeness.

Isaiah 52:13-14 (NIV)

As Jesus hung on the cross, He became so disfigured by taking upon Himself the sins of humanity that the resulting effect rendered him almost unrecognizable as a human. There have been three times in my life where Jesus has supernaturally revealed Himself to me through visions as the Suffering Savior. When I saw Him in this role, it left me afterward in speechless wonder of how much He endured to redeem us from our sins.

The grief, suffering, and agony that He experienced for us at Calvary must be viewed from the understanding that in one moment of time, all of the sins of every person who had lived or ever would live were placed on Jesus. From the smallest sins that some mistakenly consider being inconsequential to those most atrocious and shameful sins that anyone would abhor, all of them were funneled into our sinless Redeemer in one moment of time when He was on the cross. This produced an expression of agony and sorrow upon His face that is almost impossible to describe. The suffering we rightfully deserved because of our sins was put on Him so that we, through faith in Him, can be free. Only the believer in Jesus is free from the required punishment, which God's justice requires for having broken His laws. Outside of Jesus, there is no other hope or remedy for sin.

> He grew up before him like a tender shoot,
>
> and like a root out of dry ground.
>
> He had no beauty or majesty to attract us to him,
>
> nothing in his appearance that we should desire him.
>
> Isaiah 53:2 (NIV)

There have been occasions when the Lord has stood directly before me in visions in which I have clearly seen Him. Each time I have noticed there is nothing exceptional about His appearance from a physical standpoint. For decades, we have seen various movie actors who have played the role of Jesus in certain films, and the actor portraying Jesus is often handsome and attractive. While a film director has to use a certain degree of creative license to present an actor that in their mind fits the role of whom they are casting, in reality, the actors who have been selected to portray Jesus are often quite different from how He actually looks. This is not said to critique any movie promoting the message and ministry of Jesus because we should utilize every platform of spreading the gospel, especially the producing of God-honoring movies.

As a man, Jesus is certainly not ugly or unattractive, but neither is He someone that we would consider to be handsome or strikingly good-looking. Most classic Italian Renaissance paintings have established a wrong mindset among those of us in the western part of the world that has unfortunately endured for generations. Many of the great painters and sculptors of that era presented Him as soft and effeminate or, on the other hand, very suave and ravishing in appearance, neither of which is correct. Some paintings of Jesus even have Him wearing robes of certain colors that were shades of color that only women wore during that time in Israel. While we do not need to see our resurrected Lord in order to believe in Him, which was the mistake Apostle Thomas made, it is, however, important to have the right mindset of what to expect concerning His appearance. Jesus looked exactly as Isaiah described Him, who said there was nothing in His physical appearance to attract us to Him.

> He was despised and rejected by mankind,
> a man of suffering, and familiar with pain.
> Like one from whom people hide their faces
> he was despised, and we held him in low esteem.
> Surely he took up our pain
> and bore our suffering,
> yet we considered him punished by God,
> stricken by him, and afflicted.
> But he was pierced for our transgressions,
> he was crushed for our iniquities;
> the punishment that brought us peace was on him,
> and by his wounds we are healed.
> We all, like sheep, have gone astray,
> each of us has turned to our own way;
> and the Lord has laid on him

the iniquity of us all.

He was oppressed and afflicted,

yet he did not open his mouth;

he was led like a lamb to the slaughter,

and as a sheep before its shearers is silent,

so he did not open his mouth.

Isaiah 53:2-7 (NIV)

The above verses are prophetic because they share supernatural future insight about the Messiah before He ever came to earth. So much of what Isaiah revealed can be plainly evidenced in the life of Jesus as recorded in the Gospels of Matthew, Mark, Luke, and John. Other Old Testament scriptures went so far as to even tell the name of the Messiah, the town in which He would be born, what tribe of Israel He would descend from, how He would be born of a virgin, how He would spend time in Egypt, where He would grow up at, where His ministry would be centered at, how He would be rejected by the religious authorities, how He would be betrayed for thirty pieces of silver, how He would die as the Passover lamb, how He would shed His blood as an atonement for the sins of the people, how He would be lifted up on a cross and everyone would look at Him, how His hands and feet would be pierced, how His clothing would be gambled for, how God would forsake Jesus because He became contaminated with our sins on the cross, how He would conquer death and be resurrected, and how He would usher in a new covenant. The prophetic details spoken by the prophets are staggering, and these few examples are only the tip of the iceberg. The evidence is overwhelming that only Jesus of Nazareth could be the Messiah due to His fulfilling of so many complex prophecies.

The Bible is a prophetic book that is inspired by a prophetic God. It reveals events before they happen; it offers covenant solutions to life's most challenging needs, all of this while constantly pointing us to eternal life in Jesus the Messiah. The spoken and written word of God are two forms of prophetic communication. You can read the Bible, and God can speak to you through a verse or a story. A verse can speak to you in such a living way that there is no difference between the verse speaking to you from the printed page of the Bible or Jesus standing there in person and saying it to you. In reality, it is the same thing. The Bible is the only book in the world that has the ability to do this because it has spiritual life.

"The words that I speak to you are spirit, and they are life" (John 6:63b).

Don't expect to read Shakespeare or flip through your local newspaper and have the same thing happen. There is no spiritual life in that type of literature. You can also hear the Word of God preached to you and receive a distinct word that is alive, and it will reverberate through your entire being. The Word can be presented through different platforms, such as written, spoken, in song, or even acted out.

The prophet Jeremiah was often required by God to visually demonstrate his prophetic declarations. God wanted there to be imagery associated with Jeremiah's prophecies so that the people had no doubt about the deep emphasis related to His message of repentance. One of the classic examples was when God told Jeremiah to wear a linen sash around his waist, walk all the way to the Euphrates River, which was 350 miles away, and hide the sash in a hole in a rock. Later, after many days the Lord instructed him to go and dig it up. When he dug it up, he discovered it was ruined and good for nothing.

Then I went to the Euphrates and dug, and I took the sash from the place where I had hidden it; and there was the sash, ruined. It was profitable for nothing.

Then the word of the LORD came to me, saying, "Thus says the LORD: 'In this manner I will ruin the pride of Judah and the great pride of Jerusalem. This evil people, who refuse to hear My words, who follow the dictates of their hearts, and walk after other gods to serve them and worship them, shall be just like this sash which is profitable for nothing.'"

Jeremiah 13:7-10

This prophetic act symbolized the close relationship between the Lord and His covenant people. God wanted Israel as a nation to cling to him just as closely as an elastic waist strap or sash would be when snuggly positioned around someone's waist. It was essential for them to be holy and obedient in order for them to be of any use to the Lord. But sadly, they failed in this respect.

In another symbolic act, Jeremiah was told to take an earthen bottle and go with some of the elders and priests to the Hinnom Valley, just south of Jerusalem. The reason for doing so was to prophesy impending destruction against Judah and Jerusalem because of their idolatry and human sacrifice of their own children.

> This is what the Lord says: "Go, buy a potter's clay jar. Take some of the elders of the people and some of the leading priests and go out to the Valley of Hinnom near the entrance of the Potsherd Gate. Proclaim there the words I speak to you. Say: Hear the word of the Lord, kings of Judah and residents of Jerusalem. This is what the Lord of Hosts, the God of Israel, says: I am going to bring such disaster on this place that everyone who hears about it will shudder because they have abandoned Me and made this a foreign place. They have burned incense in it to other gods that they, their fathers, and the kings of Judah have never known. They have filled this place with the blood of the innocent. They have built high places to Baal on which to burn their children in the fire as burnt offerings to Baal, something I have never commanded or mentioned; I never entertained the thought."
>
> Jeremiah 19:1-5 (HCSB)

Upon declaring the prophecy before the leaders, Jeremiah threw down and broke the bottle into many pieces to symbolize how the people and the city would be broken by the invading armies of Nebuchadnezzar, the king of Babylon. Child sacrifice was common among the Ammonites who lived in Canaan. They sacrificed to Molech, which was simply another name for the main pagan deity of the area, known generally as Baal. This was a direct form of devil worship. The Lord previously said to Israel before they went into the promised land of Canaan that the inhabitants were so defiled that the land was ready to vomit them out. Judah and most of the tribes of Israel never fully possessed their inheritance. Their inability to drive out the enemy proved over time to be a fatal mistake. The customs and lifestyles of the neighboring heathen nations corrupted the pure worship, morals, and values of God's people. It wasn't long before they were practicing the same form of diabolical child sacrifice worship, thus causing the very land of their inheritance to rebel against them and now vomit them out, similar to the nations before them.

Once while on tour in Israel, we drove directly by the Hinnom Valley. Our tour guide was an Israeli Jew who was a descendant of the tribe of Judah. As we drove through the valley, he pointed to the exact spot where the Israeli archeologists had discovered the bones of many Jewish infants who had been burned in the sacrificial fires of demon worship. As he explained the findings of the archeologists, he suddenly became emotionally choked up, dropped his head in grief, and was unable to talk, overwhelmed by the sorrow of what his own forefathers had done. Needless to say, it was very quiet on the bus for a while until he regained his composure.

The intention of prophecy is to inspire us to live holy, put away sin from our lives, and walk close to the Lord in obedience to His commandments.

Abortion is the sin of shedding innocent blood. There's something that God loves above everything else, and that is His love for humans. God loves babies. For a mother to murder her own unborn child is the saddest display of selfishness and cruelty. For the father who consents to the woman aborting their child is a representation of man at his worst. It is man abandoning his highest and most noble responsibility, which is to care for and protect the life of his own child. If men and women delight in killing their own little babies, then be forewarned that they would show no restraint in killing any person if they were in a society where lawlessness were given free rein. As Mother Teresa said,

But I feel that the greatest destroyer of peace today is abortion, because it is a war against the child, a direct killing of the innocent child, murder by the mother herself. And if we accept that a mother can kill even her own child, how can we tell other people not to kill one another?[37]

To support a political platform, candidate, public official, or even an influential preacher that endorses abortion is no different than living 2,900 years ago in ancient Israel and directly participating in Baal worship and the burning alive of little babies in the fires of child sacrifice. The person who supports abortion has either knowingly or unknowingly bound themselves in spiritual chains with a covenant of death. The blood of those innocent babies is not only on the hands of the doctors who have sold their souls to profit by performing these abortions, but their blood is also on the hands of anyone who legally enabled them to carry out these atrocities.

Advancing the cause of abortion through legislation that legally and financially empowers others to shed innocent blood makes one complicit in the sin of murder. The only remedy for those who have committed this iniquity is by repenting and seeking forgiveness from God.

To receive forgiveness for murdering an unborn child, a person must first repent to God for the sin of abortion, the shedding of innocent blood. Jesus is able to forgive and wash away the sin of abortion. Upon genuine, heartfelt repentance, Jesus is then able to bring full pardon of sins, supply emotional healing, and give a clean conscience to the person who has confessed and turned away from this occult practice that ancient Israel, God's own people, succumbed to.

After the breaking of the earthen bottle, God had another highly visible prophetic object lesson for Jeremiah to carry out. Jeremiah was instructed to make a yoke that animals wear and to put it around his own neck. It's difficult to imagine how heavy and uncomfortable this must have been for the prophet. He had to wear it before King Zedekiah and the leaders of Jerusalem. No doubt some people must have thought he has absolutely crazy. Jeremiah prophesied to them that if they did not voluntarily bow down and submit to the king of Babylon, like oxen in a yoke, the Lord would destroy them all. Despite the varied opinions of what those living in Judah would have thought about Jeremiah, there was still no doubt regarding the clarity which his message conveyed. Judah was going into captivity as punishment for their unrepentant sins, and nothing could prevent it from happening.

Not only was Judah going to serve the king of Babylon, but the entire area was soon coming under the dominion of Nebuchadnezzar. Jeremiah constructed and sent yokes to the kings of the surrounding nations of Edom, Moab, Tyre, and Sidon, instructing them to fully submit and serve Nebuchadnezzar.

> "And it shall be, that the nation and kingdom which will not serve Nebuchadnezzar the king of Babylon, and which will not put its neck under the yoke of the king of Babylon, that nation I will punish," says the Lord, "with the sword, the famine, and the pestilence, until I have consumed them by his hand."
>
> Jeremiah 27:8

Jeremiah must have worn his yoke for quite a length of time, for, months later, he was still wearing it when the false prophet Hananiah took the yoke off of Jeremiah's neck and broke it in the presence of the priests and all the people. Hananiah wrongly prophesied that Nebuchadnezzar's yoke over the nations would soon be broken and that all would be well in Jerusalem. The Lord certainly didn't agree with Hananiah's lies and issued an immediate rebuke.

"Go and tell Hananiah, saying, 'Thus says the Lord: "You have broken the yokes of wood, but you have made in their place yokes of iron"'" (Jeremiah 28:13).

Jeremiah also prophesied that Hananiah would die that year because he taught rebellion against the Lord. Two months later, Hananiah was dead. We must be very careful that we don't twist prophecy and attempt to use it as a platform to vent our personal frustrations or to promote a soulish or selfish agenda. The false prophet Zedekiah tried to give a convincing prophecy to Ahab, the king of Israel, that his army would triumph in the battle against the Syrians. Zedekiah even made himself a pair of iron horns and told the king, "With these you shall gore the Syrians until they are destroyed" (1 Kings 22:11). Whenever you have genuine symbolic prophetic acts, you will also have counterfeits pop up, such as Zedekiah. Similar to trying to hold to a particular party line, other prophets jumped on their popular prophetic line and also wrongly prophesied to the king regarding a military victory. It took real courage for Micaiah to prophesy truthfully that if King Ahab went into battle, he would certainly die, which was exactly opposite to what all the other prophets had spoken. Ahab refused to listen to Micaiah and had him put in prison for giving a prophecy that he didn't agree with. Ahab confidently rode off into battle, where he was soon hit between the joints of his armor by a random arrow fired from the bow of a Syrian archer. Mortally wounded, he was taken from the battlefield and died before sundown. Micaiah may not have had iron horns or other items at his disposal to add symbolism to his prophetic words, but he did understand the key thrust of prophetic ministry, which is simply being able to hear from God and to uncompromisingly share the message.

Other well-known prophets also functioned in symbolic prophetic acts. The Lord had Ezekiel cut his own hair from his head and beard, weigh it, burn some of it, strike some of it with a sword and scatter the rest in the wind. Ezekiel's hair was used to symbolize the impending judgment upon the city of Jerusalem and the three types of calamities that would befall those who lived in the city. Some were killed by fire, others by the sword, while others were scattered to distant countries.

Isaiah named both of his sons with unusual names as prophetic acts directed by God. The name of the first son was "A Remnant Shall Return." Many years later, a remnant from what was left of the Northern Kingdom of Israel did return to Judah during the reign of Hezekiah. They repented and turned to the Lord with all their hearts and celebrated Passover. Thus the name of the first son, "A

Remnant Shall Return," was fulfilled. The second son was named "Spoil Quickly, Plunder Speedily." His name was a clear reference to the exile and dispersal of the Northern Kingdom of Israel by the Assyrians. His name was also historically realized when Assyria uprooted Israel after they had besieged Samaria and captured it. Isaiah also walked around Jerusalem shirtless and barefoot for three long years. This was a sign to Judah that they could not flee to Egypt and Ethiopia to escape the Assyrian army, for those nations were destined to go into captivity as well.

In the New Testament, we continue to see symbolic acts associated with the delivery of prophecy. Agabus was a prophet who received direct messages from God and communicated them often through visual signs.

> And in these days prophets came from Jerusalem to Antioch. Then one of them, named Agabus, stood up and showed by the Spirit that there was going to be a great famine throughout all the world, which also happened in the days of Claudius Caesar.
>
> Acts 11:27-28

The phrase "showed by the Spirit" means Agabus did more than just verbally deliver a prophetic message, but he also demonstrated it through some means of acting it out. We see his style of ministry revealed more fully when he later traveled to Caesarea and caught up with Paul, who was on his way to Jerusalem.

> When he [Agabus] had come to us, he took Paul's belt, bound his own hands and feet, and said, "Thus says the Holy Spirit, 'So shall the Jews at Jerusalem bind the man who owns this belt, and deliver him into the hands of the Gentiles.'" Now when we heard these things, both we and those from that place pleaded with him not to go up to Jerusalem. Then Paul answered, "What do you mean by weeping and breaking my heart? For I am ready not only to be bound, but also to die at Jerusalem for the name of the Lord Jesus."
>
> Acts 21:11-13

Here we see clearly that Agabus not only gave a prophetic utterance but also attached a prophetic demonstration of tying up his own hands and feet to signify what would happen to Paul in Jerusalem. The purpose of the prophecy was not to dissuade Paul from going to Jerusalem but rather mentally prepare him for the heated persecution that he would face there from the Jewish religious leaders. When a prophecy is signified, it produces a double impact by first delivering the message and secondly by presenting it in an unforgettable way.

It is also possible for the Lord to use a prophet directly as a prophetic sign, as we see in the following scripture in reference to the prophet Ezekiel: "I have made you a sign to the house of Israel" (Ezekiel 12:6).

For some divine reason, the Lord has used a particularly well-known and much older prophet several times in my life during important junctures as a sign of change taking place in my ministry. Although he has never given me a personal prophecy, he has still been used by God as a prophetic sign just by his appearance alone. Once I met him at a church in California just before a major ministry transition took place that moved my ministry significantly forward in the plan of God. At another time, I ran into him on the other side of the country at a small farm supply store while buying food for my daughter's pet farm animals. He would seem to show up in the most unusual places just before an expansion took place in my ministry. Although I haven't seen him for a little while, it wouldn't surprise me if he pops up again in the future in some out-of-the-ordinary way. I believe that as we walk closely with the Lord that not only can we operate in signs and wonders, but by God's grace, we can also become a sign and wonder to others.

In light of the behavior of the prophets that we have looked at, both from the Old and New Testaments, it is needful to understand that Jesus is the head of the entire church and, therefore, certainly the head of all prophets. In other words, if these prophets performed symbolic acts associated with the utterance of prophecy, then you can be sure that the Great Prophet also operates in the same original anointing. Jesus is the most prophetic person you will ever meet. He can present things to you that will often require spending time in prayer to unravel the full meaning of what He shared. He often makes statements or presents prophetic images that are layered, and they have more than one meaning. Once, the Lord Jesus appeared to me in a vision wearing old shepherd's clothing. He looked as if he had just been out on a farm taking care of sheep for many days. He actually spoke to me about a blessing He would do for me on Christmas Day, which was a few months away. He never said anything about me becoming a pastor. But within a few months after that vision, I was led by the Holy Spirit to start a church, and I was soon taking care of spiritual sheep. He was trying to convey the pastoral calling to me through the symbolic clothing He was wearing. The blessing He had promised concerning Christmas Day also came to pass exactly as He had said. When you walk with Him closely, you can learn to quickly pick up on the prophetic nuances that He intertwines in His statements and various expressions of symbolism.

Once I was seeking the Lord for a message on New Year's Eve. There are always many of God's spiritually hungry people going into the new year who desire to know the theme or emphasis that the Lord is expressing for that particular coming year. Although I was seeking the Lord for a prophetic word for the larger body of Christ, the Lord first gave me a personal word while I was in prayer on my knees in the afternoon. Later that afternoon, He gave certain insight to me that was for the collective body, which I publicly shared later that night. But first, He said to me, "Ring in the New Year." With the help of the Holy Spirit who lives in me, I instantly knew what the Lord meant. Kelly and I had been married for over a decade, but I had never been able to buy her a wedding ring. The ring she was currently wearing was a simple ring which she had previously purchased from a small jewelry consignment shop before we were married. It was all we had, so she now wore it on her ring finger. But when the Lord told me, "Ring in the New Year," I knew that God was authorizing me with His backing to go and buy her a new wedding ring. The Holy Spirit had given me a supernatural *word of wisdom*, which is one of the nine gifts of the Spirit. While a word of knowledge deals with past or present knowledge that is supernaturally revealed, the word of wisdom is a supernatural directive from God that speaks to something you are to do in the immediate future.

Having received the prophetic word from God and having clearly understood its prophetic meaning, I then went with confident faith and took Kelly to a high-end diamond store where she could patiently look at the vast display of diamond rings that were offered. After carefully looking over the rings, she settled on a beautiful rose gold ring with gorgeous chocolate diamonds. With a composed joy, I purchased the ring for her and, in the process, completely emptied our personal savings account that had taken over one year to accumulate. But because the Lord had divinely instructed me to make the purchase, He supernaturally covered the expenditure. Within a few days, some large and unexpected personal offerings were given to me with instructions that they were not for the ministry but rather were to be applied solely for my personal use. I paid the tithe on the monies I had received, and the remaining money was placed into our savings account, causing our account to be completely replenished back to the exact amount of where it had been before. To my astonishment, the Lord paid for the ring.

You may be thinking, *Why didn't the Lord just tell you to go and purchase for your wife a new wedding ring?* In some instances, He does speak in such direct terms, but other times He chooses to do it differently because He desires for us to grow and develop in our prophetic understanding. Often He intentionally attaches symbolic phrases to His instructions so that we are required to train our spiritual ears to detect the full will and desire of God. After Jesus's crucifixion and resurrection, the Lord spoke to Peter with prophetic foreshadowing concerning Peter's future martyrdom.

> "Very truly I tell you, when you were younger you dressed yourself and went where you wanted; but when you are old you will stretch

out your hands, and someone else will dress you and lead you where you do not want to go." Jesus said this to indicate the kind of death by which Peter would glorify God. Then he said to him, "Follow me!"

John 21:18-19 (NIV)

Notice that Jesus indicated what type of death Peter would one day experience. The word "indicate" in the original Greek language is the word *semaino*. It means "to signify, to express and make known through a sign." This is the same word used to describe how the prophet Agabus employed a prophetic act to connect his viewers with his prophecies as recorded in the book of Acts. Tradition says that Peter was crucified upside down in Rome during one of Emperor Nero's persecutions in the first century. The early church historian Eusebius wrote

> Peter seems to have preached in Pontus and Galatia and Bithynia and Cappadocia and Asia, to the Jews of the Dispersion, and at last, having come to Rome, he was crucified head downward, for so he himself had asked to suffer.[38]

Jesus knew the martyrdom that Peter would one day suffer. At this moment in time, Peter's death was still some distance off. Jesus told Peter these things would happen, "when you are old."

A person may ask, "Why didn't Jesus just directly tell Peter that one day he would be crucified upside down?" When Jesus signified this to Peter, we don't know what type of facial expression the Lord had. We don't know if he used His arms or hands to make certain motions. But regardless of the Lord's method of delivery, there's no doubt that Peter understood the message being conveyed. Peter knew that the world had been turned upside down by sin. As an apostle of the Lamb, he poured out his life to make known to Jews and Gentiles that Jesus had made provision for sin through His atoning sacrifice for all who would receive Him by faith. When Peter hung on the cross upside down, he actually saw the world in its proper perspective. As heathens said of the early apostles, "These who have turned the world upside down have come here too" (Acts 17:6). Sometimes you have to view things from a different position in order to really see the truth, even if that means viewing it from an upside-down inverted angle.

When the Holy Spirit manifests a supernatural fragrance to you, it is important to identify the prophetic meaning of what you are smelling. Supernatural fragrance is a prophetic sign from God. It is the Lord endeavoring to reveal an important message to you. Some Christians have shared with me over the years that at various times they have smelled in the spiritual realm, but even though they can identify the *type* of scent, they are unable to decipher the *meaning* of the smell. Not understanding the meaning of the scent is like reading a road sign in a foreign language that you aren't familiar with. Trying to guess what the road sign actually means is not a good idea. It could be a warning of a dangerous turn ahead and that you need to slow down, or it could mean that you can safely increase your speed because you just exited a construction zone. If we don't know what the sign means, then we need to stop and find out. Assuming that we are correct when we are actually wrong can lead to setbacks and disappointments.

When I was young and just starting off in ministry, I wanted to move forward on a certain ministry project prematurely. Even though my timing was wrong, I kept persisting in my efforts. Kelly kindly told me that she thought the timing wasn't right for what I was trying to do. Despite her concern, I pressed onward, convinced in my mind that God would bless my plan. One afternoon in the midst of my religious exuberance, I suddenly smelled bubblegum. The smell was so clear that it was as if I were standing in an invisible pink cloud of bubblegum fragrance all around me. In my zeal, I interpreted this as a positive prophetic sign, meaning my plan was going to "successfully increase and blow up, like when chewing bubblegum and blowing a big bubble." Well, my plan soon fell apart and came to nothing. Through prayer, I had accurately picked up in my spirit something God wanted me to do. My mistake was trying to do it before its appointed time. It wasn't until four years later that I actually stepped into the fullness of that plan. I had stepped out prematurely and gotten ahead of God, which is never the correct place to be in. If we are out in front of Him, we can't see Him. He is supposed to be out in front of us, leading as we follow. Just because we are willing to do good work for the Lord doesn't mean God commissions or endorses the work. The commission to do certain work and the timing of when it is to occur must both be in the perfect will of God.

"Unless the Lord builds the house, the builders labor in vain" (Psalm 127:1a).

I didn't know then what I have come to know now, that the supernatural fragrance of bubblegum consistently represents immature behavior. Children and teens love bubblegum. But when you mature, you eventually move past that stage. God is patient; He knows that there are some things we will only learn through growth and grace, and He smiles as He sees our forward progress. If I had been more sensitive to the Holy Spirit, I would have realized that my timing was incorrect, regardless of whether the gift of discerning of spirits was in operation or not, which allowed me to smell bubblegum.

While it is necessary for us to be active in our faith and have a desire to see the promises of God come to pass, we must also be patient. We possess the promises of God through faith and patience. It's good for us to enjoy the journey and not just live for the moment when we reach our destination. When you begin to understand the prophetic language of heavenly fragrance, you step into a more effective place of ministry toward others, as well as accurately making sound decisions that agree with the wisdom and counsel of God. If we try to rush God, it reveals that we are accusing Him of being at fault for not causing things to happen when we want them to. This can be the case especially for ministers who feel the call of God to full-time ministry. While the calling may be genuine, it takes time for the Lord to develop a Christian to stand effectively in a five-fold ministry office, whether that office is apostle, prophet, evangelist, pastor, or teacher.

There is always a preparation period in which a foundation of biblical truth is laid. If you go too soon, then you go on your own.

If God doesn't send you out, you are sending yourself out in your own limited power and resources. But when God sends you, He is responsible for not only supplying the anointing and empowerment for you to fill a ministry office but also supplying for your financial needs. Consider the following verse: "And He said to them, 'When I sent you without money bag, knapsack, and sandals, did you lack anything?' So they said, 'Nothing'" (Luke 22:35).

I have seen certain Christians try to step into full-time ministry without God's commissioning, and they struggle in all areas. Things just don't seem to ever come together for them, and this is true for their finances as well. But if God calls you and sends you, then He is obligated to take care of you. When the Lord called me into full-time ministry, I was working in a salaried position for forty-eight hours per week with a well-known corporation. One morning, the Holy Spirit spoke to me in my prayer time and said, "Today, when you go into work, turn in your two-week notice, you are going full-time into the ministry." That morning, when I told the general manager of my decision, he replied by saying, "Steven, are you sure you want to do that? This morning we had discussed among the leadership team and unanimously decided that we want you to become the manager over the entire department you have been working in." With much respect and appreciation, I thanked him not only for the offer but for the enjoyable years I had spent working with such a great company.

Two weeks later, I stepped full-time into the itinerant prophetic ministry, with only three upcoming meetings booked on my schedule for the entire year. But because the Lord sent me, I am able to respond affirmatively to the same question asked of the apostles by the Lord, "When I sent you...did you lack anything?" Kelly and I have certainly had our challenging times over the years when our faith has been tested and difficult circumstances stood before us. But through it all, God proved Himself faithful, and we, too, can say, "We have lacked nothing." Jesus knew and understood the principle that divine provision is tied to divine commission. You can't commission yourself, only God can send you, and only He can anoint you for service. Because Jesus was on a divine commission, we see that provision was always flowing into His ministry.

> Now it came to pass, afterward, that He went through every city and village, preaching and bringing the glad tidings of the kingdom of God. And the twelve were with Him, and certain women who had been healed of evil spirits and infirmities—Mary called Magdalene, out of whom had come seven demons, and Joanna the wife of Chuza, Herod's steward, and Susanna, and many others who provided for Him from their substance.
>
> Luke 8:1-3

If you feel that God has a calling on your life into the ministry, stay faithful, allow Him to prepare you, study the Scriptures, pray diligently, be patient, and at the right time, He will commission you into the ministry office that He has planned for you. We all have a part to play in seeing the fulfillment of the Great Commission. Whether you are a five-fold minister or a Mary, Johanna, or Susanna who generously supported the Lord's ministry through their financial support, or one of the "many others" who also contributed financially, we all must put forth our very best to see that every person on the earth has the opportunity to hear the gospel message shared with them. The decision of what a person does with the Gospel when they hear it comes down to their choice, but we must do all we can to present that choice to them in a clear and effective way. When we do our best, you can be assured that countless numbers of them will choose to depart from spiritual death and accept Christ. All over the world, people will come to know that He is the only true God who is to be worshipped in spirit and truth.

"For from the rising of the sun to its setting my name will be great among the nations, and in every place incense will be offered to my name" (Malachi 1:11a, ESV).

A Fragrance Fit for a King

"His delight is in the fear of the LORD, and He shall not judge by the sight of His eyes, nor decide by the hearing of His ears" (Isaiah 11:3).

In the eleventh chapter of the book of Isaiah, we see listed the seven spirits of the Lord. The prophet Isaiah lived in Israel around seven hundred years before Jesus was born. In this portion of the Scripture, Isaiah revealed that when the coming Messiah would appear, He would function in a seven-fold anointing of the Holy Spirit. Jesus functioned as a regular man who ministered in great power because the Holy Spirit rested upon Him. There is only one Holy Spirit, but he is best described through seven primary attributes. One of those attributes is the fear of the Lord. Referring to Jesus, it was foretold that He would *delight* in the fear of the Lord. The word "delight" in Hebrew is very interesting because, in this context, it means "scent" or "smell." When Jesus stepped into His earthly ministry, there were times when the Holy Spirit allowed Him to perceive and discern the hearts of men through smell. This supernatural ability made Him delightfully quick and sharp in the fear of the Lord. The Jewish sages have always been well aware of the valuable role that God established through spiritual smell, as seen by the commentary of Isaiah 11:3 by Ibn Ezra, a Jewish biblical commentator who lived in the twelfth century in Spain.

> The ear is sometimes deceived in hearing sounds, which are only imaginary; the eye, too, sees things in motion, which in reality are at rest; the sense of smell alone is not deceived. He will properly investigate the question before him by his piety; he will not judge according to what he seems to see or to hear, because the testimony of the witnesses might be false.[39]

In the end times, we are going to see levels of deceit and fraud expressed in all forms of media in an attempt to deceive and mislead people. Technology in the movie, television, and video industry has become so advanced that programmers can use certain software that enables them to take video footage of someone's head and face and place it on the head of another person. Voice editing is then added, a different background is keyed in, and the software makes it appear that the featured person is doing and saying a certain thing, but it is only an illusion, a cleverly designed lie. This type of video editing is known to programmers as a "Deep Fake." But the Holy Spirit can never be faked, and neither can you when you are walking closely with God. The Holy Spirit can reveal when someone or some group is lying to you. He can expose the lie by manifesting a supernatural smell to warn you of the deception. Understanding this manifestation of the Spirit will become even more important in the end times because we may visually see events that are played before us on news presentations, but what we view could be fake. As Rabbi Ibn Ezra said, "The sense of smell alone is not deceived." Jesus could judge by supernatural smell, and there can be times when you will as well, through the manifestation of the Holy Spirit.

As humans, we have five physical senses, which give us the ability to see, hear, taste, touch, and smell. But of the five, perhaps smell is the most honest of our senses. The ability to smell in the spiritual realm in order to make correct judgments was expected of the Messiah, according to various Jewish experts of the Old Testament. Rava the Sage (a rabbi who lived in Babylon in the fourth century) is mentioned in the Babylonian Talmud (a commentary on the Old Testament) as having said that the Messiah King would be anointed with a special gift that would enable Him to make correct judgments through His ability to smell.[40] With a scriptural basis (Isaiah 11:3) for this belief, the Talmud comments on a man named Shimon Bar Kokhba. He was the leader of the Jewish rebellion in the year AD 132, in which Jerusalem and Judea were regained for a short time. But the power and the enormous size of the Roman army proved to be too much for Bar Kokhba's men, and within three years, the revolt was overthrown. In an effort to further destroy the Jewish culture and identity, Judea was renamed Palaestinia (a name that, unfortunately, many still use to wrongly identify the land of Israel), and Jerusalem was changed to Aelia Capitolina. Bar Kokhba had been regarded by many Jews as the Messiah, but it is said that he failed to pass the test of being able to judge by smell, and that is why he was killed. The story of Bar Kokhba being unable to satisfy the request of the sages to discern justice through smell is said by some rabbis to be a legend. However, one thing the legend does prove is that Jewish religious scholars were aware of the meaning of Isaiah 11:3, and they expected the Messiah to be able to meet this high standard foretold by the prophet Isaiah.

Well-known evangelical theologians have also spoken about this unique anointing that Jesus would function in, as we see from the commentary of John Calvin, the French theologian, pastor, and reformer from the sixteenth century. Commenting on Isaiah 11:3, he states:

> The verb *rych*, (riach) which is here put in the Hiphil conjugation, signifies literally to smell; but may also be explained in an active sense, as meaning to give a keen smell; which agrees better, I think, with this passage, so that this sagacity may be also included among the gifts of the Spirit. And this effect is peculiarly applicable to the person of Christ, namely, that far beyond what the godly are able to conceive, he is endowed with shrewd discernment for governing his people. We ought to attend, first of all, to the metaphor in the verb smell, which means that Christ will be so shrewd that he will not need to learn from what he hears, or from what he sees; for by smelling alone he will perceive what would otherwise be unknown.[41]

In the above quote, John Calvin directly said that the Lord's ability to spiritually smell is to be included among the gifts of the Spirit. This harmonizes with the gifts of the Spirit mentioned in the book of 1 Corinthians 12:1-11, which reveals the nine gifts of the Holy Spirit. Among the nine gifts, we see the gift of discerning of spirits, which is the ability to see, hear, taste, touch, and *smell* in the spiritual realm. In the spirit realm, the five senses can function at a much higher level than the physical realm.

"But the manifestation of the Spirit is given to each one for the profit of all; for to one is given the [...] discerning of spirits" (1 Corinthians 12:7, 10).

Discerning of spirits includes discernment in the realm of evil spirits, which would consist of demons and even Satan himself. The spirit realm also involves holy angels, redeemed saints, and God. We can also take human spirits into account because if the Holy Spirit is manifesting this gift, then we can know human intents and motives. This gift so often reveals insights into operations going on behind the scenes that our natural and mental senses would not be capable of knowing.

Some well-meaning biblical commentators, in an effort to explain this supernatural gift, have identified it as the "gift of discernment" instead of using the biblical term "gift of discerning of spirits." However, there is no mention in the Bible of a gift of discernment. Discernment is not a gift, nor is it supernatural. According to dictionary.com, *discernment* is the ability to recognize small details, accurately tell the difference between similar things, and make intelligent judgments by using such observations.[42] For example, in the following scripture, we see that God equates discernment primarily with *distinguishing the difference between what is morally right and morally wrong*.

> And should I not pity Nineveh, that great city, in which are more than one hundred and twenty thousand persons who cannot discern between their right hand and their left—and much livestock?
>
> Jonah 4:11

God's Word, the Bible, is the guidebook and highest authority for discernment. The ancient citizens of Nineveh had no accurate moral compass to guide them. However, through Jonah's preaching, they repented of their wicked ways, and we see that God actually displayed great compassion toward them by sparing their city from destruction. When you conduct your life in the light of God's Word, your discernment between right and wrong will become very sharp.

Most of the incorrect views concerning discerning of spirits can originate from not understanding that this is a supernatural gift. You can't make the gift of discerning of spirits fit into the category of the intellectual realm or the mental realm. This gift should be kept in its proper category of being a supernatural gift. When the wonderful fragrances of heaven are being emitted, it means the anointing of God's Spirit is working in the lives of those present. Whether the fragrance is good, bad, sweet, or something that smells awful, we need to seek the Lord for the meaning of what we are experiencing. There is a certain fragrance that comes forth in my meetings when there is a high level of God's anointing that is present to work miracles. When I pray for a person and a creative miracle happens, I have discovered that this specific fragrance is always manifested. The smell is very thick and oily; it is not a high sweet floral smell, but more on the low bass end toward some type of a mixture of musk and amber. It is a very pleasing smell, but it is not something I can fully identify.

Once, while I was in Israel, I was asked to pray for a teenage boy who had flat feet. His mother told me he was born with no arches in his feet. The boy was fourteen years old. At this time, I had just finished praying for about 200 sick people. Most of the people had left except for a small group of about twenty people. Suddenly I began to smell the heavenly musk fragrance. The moment I smelled the fragrance, I *knew* God was with me in a special way. This *knowing* created a tremendous surge of faith in my heart. It's like having a gust of wind fill your sails, a divine push from heaven that lets you know that you can step out in faith. With bold confidence, I asked those remaining, "How many of you would like to see a miracle?" They all responded in the positive. I said, "Then come close and watch what God is going to do!" I asked the young boy to sit down and take off his shoes and socks so that we could all see the miracle. I held one of his feet in my hands, and I was going to pray for him using the authority of the name of Jesus. But before I could even pray a short prayer, I could feel the bones in his foot moving. Within three seconds, a perfectly formed arch appeared in his foot. I took the other foot and held it in my hands, and it also had an arch appear in less than five seconds. The whole time this was taking place, I could smell that specific heavenly musk fragrance.

Because I am a minister, the Lord uses fragrances as a spiritual indicator of when I should step out in faith and minister to those in need. My apostolic spiritual father has operated in many miracles and healings around the world. In a discussion we once had about yielding to the Holy Spirit in order to minister to others, he shared that as he preached his sermon, he would sometimes begin to *feel* like he was wearing a *baseball cap*. As the cap would begin to feel tighter and tighter, his faith would begin to grow stronger and stronger. When the cap felt extremely tight, he would then stop preaching and begin to lay hands on the sick, and God would then perform miracles. The ways of the Holy Spirit are wonderful. It is important for you to spend time with God and discover your own methods of effective ministry.

The gift of discerning of spirits often accompanies those who are called by God into the ministry office of the prophet. While this gift can be experienced by any believer, it often functions in a higher capacity in the ministry office of the prophet. Jesus flowed in all nine of the gifts of the Spirit, so there's no question He had the gift of discerning of spirits. He could clearly smell in the spiritual realm when the anointing came upon Him because He was filled with the Spirit without measure. When the anointing of the Spirit came upon Jesus, He would be able to discern things spiritually through smell. We also see in Scripture that the spiritual garments of Jesus were scented.

"All Your garments are scented with myrrh and aloes and cassia, Out of the ivory palaces, by which they have made You glad" (Psalm 45:8a).

The words "are scented" are not in the original Hebrew; they were added by the English translators in an effort to give us a smooth and understandable reading experience. But the Hebrew language is very clear in revealing that the various fragrances of myrrh, aloes, and cassia are so profuse that they themselves are, in a figure, the garments that the Lord wears. This spiritual bouquet of fragrance that exuded from the Lord was a sign of His kingly status. In the ancient Middle East, a king could easily be identified not only by his wealth and vast possessions but also through the scent of opulent fragrant oils that were poured on him. Back then, you would know when a king was passing by not only seeing his large promenade of servants and armed guards but also because of the thick fragrance of exotic oils which he wore that filled the air. At the coronation of Israel's kings, they would be anointed with holy oil. The oil was perfumed with spices that were very expensive, thus making the oil a symbol of wealth, rarity, and exclusivity. The oil was never just placed upon anyone randomly, but whoever the oil was placed upon was considered to be set apart for the special purposes of God.

> So Zadok the priest, Nathan the prophet, Benaiah the son of Jehoiada, the Cherethites, and the Pelethites went down and had Solomon ride on King David's mule, and took him to Gihon. Then Zadok the priest took a horn of oil from the tabernacle and anointed Solomon. And they blew the horn, and all the people said, "Long live King Solomon!" And all the people went up after him; and the people played the flutes and rejoiced with great joy, so that the earth seemed to split with their sound.
>
> 1 Kings 1:38-40

Although the kings of Israel were not crowned during a coronation, the highly fragrant oil produced a crowning effect upon the king's head. Some call it the "halo effect" in which the illuminated glory of God can be seen upon the head and face of the person who has been anointed. The fragrant oil was a type and shadow in the Old Testament that symbolized the empowerment of the Holy Spirit that we now experience in the New Testament. In a Mother's Day service in 1993, my former pastor once had his mother speak on Sunday morning to the church. As his mother spoke, her face became so illuminated that countless people in the service, including myself, could see brilliant rays of light streaming out of her face. I found out a few days later that just before she spoke, she had completed a lengthy fast coupled with much prayer. Needless to say, she was heavily anointed. Another time, I was hosting a Christian businessmen's luncheon when an international evangelist unexpectedly came to my meeting. We were friends, but I hadn't seen him in over a year. When Kelly and I saw him walk in, we instantly discussed with one another the astonishing fact that light was emanating from his face. He sat next to me while we had our lunch together. I leaned over and whispered to him, "Rod, did you know that your face is beaming with a heavenly light?" Eating a small salad, he smiled and humbly said, "I just finished three days of prayer and fasting, having drunk only water during my fast." Sitting there next to him, I actually started to feel somewhat inebriated because of the glory of God that was resting upon him and which was radiating over on me. It is vitally important that we be crowned with the fragrant oil of the Holy Spirit so that we can minister in the power of the Holy Spirit to others.

Once I was ministering in India, and they brought into the church meeting a young woman in her early twenties. I was told by the associate pastor that she was blind, demon-possessed, and in a vegetative mental state. This woman was placed on the front row of the audience seating area. She lay over on the chairs in a crumpled position; to me, she appeared similar to a sack of potatoes, having no control over her body and in a listless condition. After I finished my preaching session, I began to lay my hands on the sick and pray for their healing. With the help of several assistants, they carried the woman to me, and I laid my hands on her head and cast out the evil spirit in the name of Jesus. They carried her away, and it didn't appear that anything had changed in her, but I was confident that the anointing of the Holy Spirit had flowed into her body. It is the anointing of the Spirit that removes burdens and destroys yokes that the devil places on people.

The next morning was the main Sunday service, and the church was packed with several thousand people. The time of praise and worship was beautiful. As the last worship song was concluding, everyone there was high in faith and enjoying the rich presence of God. There was a side curtain through which people could enter and exit the sanctuary during the meeting. At the moment in which the high worship concluded, the side curtain opened and the young woman who had been carried into the meeting the night before stepped into the sanctuary and began walking under her own power toward the front of the sanctuary. She walked with such regality and grace that it seemed like she was gliding over the floor. But her face told the greatest story. Streams of light were flooding out of her face. The church was stunned; gasps could be heard everywhere. The pastor was standing when he saw her come through the curtain, and he almost stumbled and fell when he initially saw her because of the shock of seeing such a change. Composing himself, he quickly ran to her and escorted her up on the platform for everyone to see the miracle that Jesus had done for her. She could walk, she could see clearly with her eyes, and she had no pain in her body. The demon was gone, and she had invited Jesus into her heart to be her Lord and Savior.

Before she was brought to the church service, she had been a Muslim, but now she belonged to Jesus. After her testimony, I ministered to the people, and God's power continued to heal and deliver many. Not only was God healing His own people, but in His mercy, He was also healing Hindus and Muslims who were reaching out in faith to receive. The fragrances of God were manifesting so strongly in the meetings that it almost seemed like you were going to be swept away by the heavenly perfumes. Everyone could smell them. The Lord does these things to reveal His glory, His goodness, and His desire to save, refresh, heal, and deliver all who put their trust in Him.

"And when Jesus was in Bethany at the house of Simon the leper, a woman came to Him having an alabaster flask of very costly fragrant oil, and she poured it on His head as He sat at the table" (Matthew 26:6-7).

Jesus explained to His disciples that the woman intentionally poured the fragrant oil on Him for His burial. This anointing happened after His kingly triumphal entry into Jerusalem, which was two days before the Passover, just before He was crucified. This unnamed woman knew that Jesus was the Messiah, knew that He was going to soon die, and knew that He was the King of kings. Empowered with this revelation of the true identity of Jesus, she sacrificially gave from her personal treasury an alabaster flask of fragrant oil that would be like diamonds in our modern-day financial equivalent. This was not a normal anointing, this was an anointing for the upcoming burial of the great King. It took place just before He was crucified.

What is wisdom? Wisdom is the ability to recognize difference. She recognized the difference in Jesus from other men. She recognized who He really was, that He was not just another prophet, but rather the Great Prophet foretold by Moses in the Torah. He was the Messiah, the King of kings, and Lord of lords, and she acted accordingly by releasing a lavish gift fit for a king. Because of this, Jesus said her magnificent act of love, sacrifice, faith, and wisdom would be told throughout the world as a memorial to her.

It is important to understand that Jesus was the rightful king of Israel. At the time of Israel's exile to Babylon, there were no more kings of Israel, and the southern kingdom of Judah ceased to function as a nation. However, the kingly genealogy was still kept with the utmost care, as noted in Matthew's Gospel in the first chapter. All of the men listed since the captivity were firstborn sons of King David, thus recognizing them as the rightful kings of Israel. This genealogy includes Joseph, a direct descendant of David, and his son Solomon. Although the land area of Israel was under Roman subjugation around the time of 10 BC, if Israel had been a nation, then Joseph would have been the true heir to the throne. This seems difficult for some Christians to grasp because they only view Joseph as being a poor carpenter.

We know that Joseph and Mary were not wealthy because when they presented Jesus to the Lord at the temple, they could only give the poorest offering of two turtledoves or two young pigeons. One would be used as a burnt offering, the other as a sin offering as required by the Mosaic Law. This was the offering made by the poor who could not afford to give a lamb. The throne of David and the former glory of the nation of Israel had been so diminished that it appeared similar to a mighty tree that had been cut down with nothing left but an old useless stump. However, the royal lineage could be directly traced to Joseph, who, even in his humble state as a carpenter, would have been aware of his kingly lineage. This deteriorated position of status is supported by Scripture because Isaiah gave us a prophecy with the image of a slender twig or shoot sprouting up from the root of a decayed stump. The Messiah's appearance would occur against all odds and when it seemed least likely for it to happen.

"There shall come forth a shoot from the stump of Jesse, and a branch from his roots shall bear fruit" (Isaiah 11:1, ESV).

Several years after the Lord's birth, the Magi visited Him with gifts of gold, frankincense, and myrrh. These were exquisite gifts that were given to the Child King. These valuable offerings by the Magi would have elevated the financial well-being of the family to a considerable degree. Joseph and Mary were raising the Anointed One, the King of Israel, in their home. After the Lord started His ministry, there were many who recognized Him as their Messianic King. For example, blind Bartimaeus called out loudly to Jesus, saying, "Jesus, Son of David, have mercy on me!" (Mark 10:47). "Son of David" is a Jewish expression that refers to the promise God made to David that he would have an heir who would be King over Israel forever. The good news is that those who belong to Jesus are placed into a new identity in Him as kings and priests. Every believer should recognize their royal lineage in Christ and have a kingly mindset.

"And has made us kings and priests to His God and Father, to Him be glory and dominion forever and ever. Amen" (Revelation 1:6).

"And have made us kings and priests to our God; And we shall reign on the earth" (Revelation 5:10).

Can you imagine what Jesus, the King of the Jews, must have smelled like when He stood before the mock trial of the Jewish

Sanhedrin, where He was insulted, beaten, and spat upon? When he was taken to Pilate and then sent to Herod Antipas, I wonder, what they thought about the unmistakable way in which He smelled? When Pilate directly asked Him, "Are you the king of the Jews?" he must have discerned that Jesus certainly smelled like a king. When He was scourged by the Roman soldiers and then forced to carry His own cross, the flow of blood and the deep exertion of strength would have caused every pore in His body to pour out sweat and emit the previously absorbed fragrant oil. The soldiers would have noticed this as they carried out their gruesome work of scourging Him and eventually nailing Him to a cross. When they gambled for His outer garment, the winning recipient surely would have noticed the fragrance that had absorbed into the fabric of the cloth.

Everywhere He went during the final few days of His life, He would have smelled like the King that He truly was. Jesus died to redeem us from our sins and to impart His new life into us. When we put our trust in Him and accept Him as our Lord, Savior, and King, we are entitled to covenant privileges. The privileges and blessings of the new covenant enable us to walk in the victory that He purchased for us at Calvary. Victory has a pleasing fragrance that is found in the knowledge, principles, and commandments of Jesus the Messiah, the Anointed One. As believers, we rejoice in this fragrance, but to those who do not belong to Jesus, this same symbolic fragrance expressed through the good news of salvation is ridiculed. In the spiritual realm, smell cannot be hidden. The Gospel carries a spiritual fragrance that is so strong that even the unsaved can discern it.

> Thanks be to God who leads us, wherever we are, on his own triumphant way and makes our knowledge of him spread throughout the world like a lovely perfume! We Christians have the unmistakable "scent" of Christ, discernible alike to those who are being saved and to those who are heading for death. To the latter it seems like the very smell of doom, to the former it has the fresh fragrance of life itself.
>
> 2 Corinthians 2:14-16a (Phillips)

Death, decay, and defeat emit an unpleasant fragrance. The spiritual realm runs parallel to the natural realm. The plan that God has for your life does not include sickness, disease, poverty, depression, addiction, fear, confusion, or any form of defeat or humiliation.

> In the Messiah, in Christ, God leads us from place to place in one perpetual victory parade. Through us, he brings knowledge of Christ. Everywhere we go, people breathe in the exquisite fragrance. Because of Christ, we give off a sweet scent rising to God, which is recognized by those on the way of salvation—an aroma redolent with life. But those on the way to destruction treat us more like the stench from a rotting corpse.

2 Corinthians 2:14-15 (MSG)

The New Testament was originally written in Greek, which contains many "word pictures" that were understood clearly by the readers during the time in which the epistles were written. The Christians in Corinth understood the word picture that Paul was conveying here was of a Roman general parading through the streets with his victorious army and leading his defeated captives behind him in chains. Along the parade route, flowers were offered to the conquering general, and incense and spices were burned in his honor. The parade ended at the Roman Colosseum, where the prisoners were forced into various forms of barbaric "entertainment" for the Roman citizens. The conquered foes were used to fight lions, tigers, and other wild animals, and some were staged as gladiators who died brutal deaths. But we are not a part of the spiritual kingdom of darkness that was defeated; rather, we belong to the victorious kingdom of light that is led by Jesus Christ, who conquered sin, death, hell, and the grave. His victory has become our victory. His fragrance has become our fragrance.

We should examine ourselves to make sure that we are drenched with the perfume of Jesus. I'm not referring to wearing cologne or perfume, but I'm saying this from a spiritual perspective. When we live in close fellowship with God, His life flows into us. Spending time with God is like putting on a nice perfume before heading out for the day. The fragrance makes you happy, but others notice it as well. As we soak in His presence, our garments will also become scented, and we will begin to smell like Jesus. You may work at a fish factory where all day long you fillet fish and even smell like them at the end of the day, but the spiritual fragrance of who you belong to (Jesus) remains strongest on you. You may be a garbage collector and are around foul smells all day, but the fragrance of Christ still rests upon you because you are a child of God. There was a season in my life when I worked as a plumber. I would crawl beneath houses and get extremely dirty, and often my work environment smelled bad, but because I loved the Lord, I could still minister to people even in the midst of such unpleasant circumstances. The Lord is concerned about the aroma that emanates from our hearts.

"Some men are good smelling and some are stinking to God"[43] (John Wycliffe, theologian and Bible translator of the fourteenth century).

The outside of the body can be easily cleaned up with a hot shower and soap, but the inside is where we should focus our attention. After His resurrection, Jesus appeared to Mary in the form of a humble servant, and she couldn't recognize Him. She actually thought she was talking to the gardener. In the twelfth century, Saint Francis was riding his horse near Assisi when he met a man with leprosy. The sight and putrid smell of the leper filled him with an initial disgust, but Francis got off his horse and hugged and kissed the leper. The leper put out his hand, wanting to receive something. Francis gave money to the leper and then got back up on his horse, at which point Francis noticed the leper was nowhere in sight. Although the plain lay open and clear on all sides with no obstacles in sight, yet he still could not see the leper anywhere. It was then he realized it was Jesus that he had kissed.

A fragrant heart full of the love of God reaches out to everyone regardless of how they may look or smell. A saintly walk with God will always involve surprises in the various ways in which the Lord communicates with His people. What may appear to be insignificant or unattractive to us may have the Lord Himself hidden in it. We should be mindful of this, especially in the area of smell. Just because something smells good doesn't always mean it has God's approval, and just because something smells bad doesn't mean it should frighten us away. Let us be led by the Holy Spirit so that we always recognize Jesus, whether He is presented to us in royal robes drenched in myrrh, aloes, and cassia, or should He come disguised in beggar's garments appearing as a foul-smelling homeless man. The condition of our heart will determine our response. May it be a fragrant response that flows out of your heart.

Prayer, Holy Incense, and the House of Avtinas

And the Lord said to Moses: "Take sweet spices, stacte and onycha and galbanum, and pure frankincense with these sweet spices; there shall be equal amounts of each. You shall make of these an incense, a compound according to the art of the perfumer, salted, pure, and holy. And you shall beat some of it very fine, and put some of it before the Testimony in the tabernacle of meeting where I will meet with you. It shall be most holy to you. But as for the incense which you shall make, you shall not make any for yourselves, according to its composition. It shall be to you holy for the Lord. Whoever makes any like it, to smell it, he shall be cut off from his people."

Exodus 30:34-38

Aaron shall burn on it sweet incense every morning; when he tends the lamps, he shall burn incense on it. And when Aaron lights the lamps at twilight, he shall burn incense on it, a perpetual incense before the Lord throughout your generations.

Exodus 30:7-8

The priests were the descendants of Aaron and were from the tribe of Levi. Each day at the temple, there were many required assignments that the priests had to complete. They were responsible for teaching the people of Israel the laws of God, they officiated at the temple sacrifices, and they blessed the people and put God's name upon them. The Levites assisted the priests in the temple work. They performed the maintenance and construction for the temple, they guarded the temple day and night, and some were skilled musicians, others excellent singers. However, only the priests, the *kohanim*, were allowed to minister the most sacred tasks of worship in the Holy Place. According to 1 Chronicles 23, it was King David who divided all the priests and Levites, separated them by their families, and assigned them their tasks in the temple.

Within the Holy Place of the temple, there were three primary pieces of sacred furniture. The first piece of furniture a priest would notice when coming into the Holy Place would be the golden lampstand, also called the *menorah*, which stood toward the left of the altar of incense. It was hammered out of one piece of solid gold. The lampstand had a middle branch from which three branches extended upward on each side, making a total of seven branches. On top of each branch was a cuplike lamp that held olive oil and a wick. The seven lamps that were atop the menorah represent the seven spirits of the Lord. These seven spirits are the seven primary attributes of the Holy Spirit. As mentioned in Isaiah, chapter eleven, verses 1–3, they are:

1. The Spirit of the Lord
2. The Spirit of Wisdom
3. The Spirit of Understanding
4. The Spirit of Counsel
5. The Spirit of Might
6. The Spirit of Knowledge
7. The Spirit of the Fear of the Lord

Pictured is a reconstruction of the seven-lamp Temple menorah created by the Temple Institute in Jerusalem, Israel

The pure olive oil that was burned on the menorah was a type of the Holy Spirit, who is the third Person of the blessed Trinity. The priests lit the menorah every evening and cleaned it out every morning. In the morning cleaning process, the wicks would be replaced and fresh olive oil would refill the cups. The lampstand stayed lit continually, and it was the only source of light in the sanctuary. Without this light, the priests would not have been able to see what they were doing. The menorah was sculpted in a beautiful way. Each branch of the menorah was designed to look like that of an almond tree, engraved with buds, blossoms, and flowering petals. Today the menorah is the national symbol of Israel, which is a reference to Israel's calling to be a light to the nations by bringing the Old Testament scriptures to the world. Christians around the world see the menorah as representing Jesus the Messiah who fulfilled the law and has become the light of the world, as foretold by Isaiah the prophet:

> I, the Lord, have called You in righteousness,
>
> And will hold Your hand;
>
> I will keep You and give You as a covenant to the people,
>
> As a light to the Gentiles,
>
> To open blind eyes,
>
> To bring out prisoners from the prison,
>
> Those who sit in darkness from the prison house.
>
> Isaiah 42:6-7

The second piece of sacred furniture in the Holy Place was the table of showbread, which is referred to as the "bread of His Presence" because it was always to be in the Lord's presence.

> And you shall take fine flour and bake twelve cakes with it. Two-tenths of an ephah shall be in each cake. You shall set them in two rows, six in a row, on the pure gold table before the Lord. And you shall put pure frankincense on each row, that it may be on the bread for a memorial, an offering made by fire to the Lord.
>
> Leviticus 24:5-7

Priests in the Holy Temple, replacing the showbread for the week

The table of showbread was toward the right of the altar of incense. It was directly opposite the menorah. The table was made of acacia wood and overlaid with gold. An elegant rim of gold was placed around the edge of the table, most likely to keep things from rolling off of it. Poles were attached so that priests could carry the table without touching it directly. The table held twelve loaves of bread which represented the twelve tribes of Israel. The twelve loaves were set out in two stacks of six loaves each. The two rows of six cakes represent that the tribes were divided in half during the times when they would assemble themselves on the two separate mountains, which were Mount Gerizim and Mount Ebal. The two mountains represented the two aspects of the law which were the blessing for the obedient and the dreadful cursing for the disobedient.

The priests baked the bread with the finest of semolina flour that had been sifted many times, and a few secret ingredients were included that caused the bread to never mold nor become stale or dry, even though the bread was exposed to the open air for a full week. Each loaf weighed about eleven pounds.

The two-tenths of an *ephah* speaks of the double-portion blessing for those Christians who enjoy encountering the Lord in the Holy Place. The Holy Place is symbolic of the church, also called the church of the firstborn (Hebrews 12:23). According to Torah law

(Deuteronomy 21:17), the firstborn gets a double portion. In other words, if a father has five sons, then the father splits the inheritance into six portions, and the oldest son gets two portions, and the other sons each get a single portion. There was, of course, a way to include the daughters in the inheritance as well.

The bread would remain on the table before the Lord for a week before being eaten by the priests every Sabbath day. This meal took place once the afternoon sacrifice was completed. The priests were the only ones allowed to eat the showbread, and it could only be eaten in the Holy Place because the bread was holy. In the ancient Middle East, having a meal with someone was a sign of fellowship and peace. When the priests would eat the showbread, it signified that the Lord was at peace with His people. However, under the old covenant, only the priests could eat the holy bread, so we see that not every Israelite enjoyed the remarkable privilege of having a meal with God. Through the shedding of His precious blood upon the cross of Calvary, Jesus has established a new covenant whereby those who put their faith and trust in Him receive eternal peace between them and God. We are now able to eat in His presence, especially when we receive communion and partake of the body and blood of Christ, our Savior. As we eat the Bread of Life, we do more than just share the gospel message—we become the message.

The third piece of holy furniture in the sanctuary was the golden altar of incense. It sat in front of the gorgeous multicolored blue, purple, and crimson veil that separated the Holy Place from the Holy of Holies. Like the table of showbread, it, too, was made of acacia wood and overlaid with gold. The wood symbolizes the humanity of Jesus. The gold represents the divinity of Jesus. Jesus is both fully God and fully man. The altar of incense was just over three feet high and was the shape of a square, with each side measuring a foot and a half.

The high priest offering incense on the golden altar.
This illustration is from Henry Davenport Northrop,
Treasures of the Bible, published in 1894

The altar of incense had four horns in each top corner that protruded outward from the altar. The priest sprinkled the horns with the blood of the sin offering in order to remove sins that were committed unintentionally. All of these details were a shadow in the Old Testament of the good things that would one day come. Those old shadows have now been fulfilled through Jesus by the shedding of His blood to make atonement for our sins. Good times are here indeed because Jesus has become our High Priest, and we have received eternal life and forgiveness of all of our sins, both intentional and unintentional sins, through Him.

The four horns on the altar speak of power in prayer. Horns in Scripture represent power. When the prophet Habakkuk spoke of *rays* of light flashing from the hand of God, we find in the original Hebrew that the word for "rays" is the word "horns." This is the secret place where God's power was hidden.

"His splendor was like the sunrise; rays flashed from his hand, where his power was hidden" (Habakkuk 3:4, NIV).

Jacob serves as a leading example in the Old Testament of a man who represented the power of prayer. When he wrestled with the Lord, the Lord said to him, "Your name shall no longer be called Jacob, but Israel; for you have struggled with God and with men, and have prevailed" (Genesis 32:28). There is tremendous power in prayer. Through prayer, we can move the mountain-type problems we face and overcome all obstacles that appear in our lives.

There was a crown of gold that went around the top of the altar of incense, which would keep the coals and the incense from falling off. Lower down on each side, there were golden rings to insert the two poles used to lift and carry the altar. The two poles were made of acacia wood and overlaid with gold. The golden rings and golden poles symbolize the truth that prayer carries us into the presence of God.

The incense that was used was a mixture of a number of rich and rare spices, some of which have been difficult to identify for the last few centuries. The remaining spices that have not yet been positively identified have in modern times undergone a high-tech chemical analysis using what is called "gas chromatography–mass spectrometry." This technology has helped modern-day scholars and scientific researchers probe further into the difficult questions surrounding the true identity of these spices and plants of antiquity. We also have as our guide the trusted writings of the Jewish sages and rabbis over the centuries who commented on the ingredients and the meaning of the *ketoret*, the holy incense offering. However, we are still left with no absolute certainty on the true identity of some of the incense ingredients, particularly that of onycha. Some writers believe that onycha came from a snaillike mollusk found in the Red Sea. But the highly respected Jewish theologian Nachmanides argued that it is not possible for onycha to have been derived from a mollusk because the mollusk was listed among the unclean creatures in the Torah. Nachmanides said that the commandment concerning unclean animals that were considered an "abomination" also made them unfit for any part of service in the temple. There is also a wide latitude of opinions among Jewish sages concerning the identity of galbanum, whether it's a tree or plant. One thing all ancient writers did agree on was that galbanum smelt awful, yet when mixed with the other incense ingredients, it enhanced and wakened their overall spicy essence.

These spices were blended with frankincense and beaten to a fine powder, and then salt was added. It was strictly forbidden for this formula to be used by any private individual. It had to be used only in the worship of God in the Holy Place. If anyone besides the authorized priests tried to develop a similar incense, they would be excommunicated from the covenant people of God.

> And the Lord said to Moses: "Take sweet spices, stacte and onycha and galbanum, and pure frankincense with these sweet spices; there shall be equal amounts of each. You shall make of these an incense, a compound according to the art of the perfumer, salted, pure, and holy. And you shall beat some of it very fine, and put some of it before the Testimony in the tabernacle of meeting where I will meet with you. It shall be most holy to you. But as for the incense which you shall make, you shall not make any for yourselves, according to its composition. It shall be to you holy for the Lord. Whoever makes any like it, to smell it, he shall be cut off from his people."
>
> Exodus 30:34-38

The priests burned incense on the golden altar once in the morning and once in the evening. God commanded that the incense was to be kept burning all day and throughout the night as a pleasing aroma to Him. Maimonides (a medieval Sephardic Jewish philosopher) writes that,

> Since many beasts were daily slaughtered in the holy place, the flesh cut in pieces and the entrails and the legs burnt and washed, the smell of the place would undoubtedly have been like the smell of the slaughterhouses, if nothing had been done to counteract it. They were therefore commanded to burn incense there twice every day, in the morning and in the evening, in order to give the place and the garments of those who officiated there a pleasant odor.

There is a well-known saying of our Sages, "In Jericho they could smell the incense" (burnt in the Temple). This provision likewise tended to support the dignity of the Temple. If there had not been a good smell, let alone if there had been a stench, it would have produced in the minds of the people the reverse of respect; for our heart generally feels elevated in the presence of good odor, and is attracted by it, but it abhors and avoids bad smell.[44]

Besides the commentary of Maimonides, the Talmud (a commentary by the distinguished rabbis on the first five books of the Bible) relates that women as far away from Jerusalem as Jericho (about twenty miles) did not wear perfumes because the fragrance emanating from the ketoret filled the air. The goats in Jericho were known to sneeze because they could smell the holy incense being burnt in Jerusalem. The incense was a symbol of the prayers and intercession of the people going up to God as a sweet fragrance. The incense was placed upon burning hot coals, which produced the fragrant aroma in the Holy Place, with the smoke being carried into the Holy of Holies. Standing in front of the altar of incense, which was directly in front of the veil, the priest would see the smoke penetrate the curtain into the Holy of Holies even though He could not see past the curtain. This is similar to how it is when we pray because as we pray, we do not actually see our prayers enter heaven, yet we still know that God hears and answers our prayers. This sacrifice further symbolized the offering of the person whose sins had been forgiven by blood and who wanted to express their love to God with thanksgiving and worship, which is what is pleasing to God's heart.

"Let my prayer be set before You as incense, The lifting up of my hands as the evening sacrifice" (Psalm 141:2).

The golden altar is a representation of the prayer life of the Lord Jesus Christ and the prayer life that He desires to lead every believer into. Jesus is our intercessor before God the Father. In a similar way in which the high priest of the tabernacle bore the names of each of the Israelite tribes on his breastplate before God, so did Jesus pray and intercede for His followers. The high priest under the old covenant would eventually die, and another qualified man would have to take his place. Jesus came to earth not only to dwell among His people in a flesh and blood body but also to fulfill the qualifications of the High Priest. The high priests under the old covenant were men who could deal gently with those who struggled with sin because they themselves were human and had their own weaknesses. The Lord was fully immersed in the human experience, which included many temptations that were presented to Him. Yet He never sinned, and this sinless status is what positioned Him to supersede the imperfect priesthood that functioned during the old covenant.

> There were many priests under the old system, for death prevented them from remaining in office. But because Jesus lives forever, his priesthood lasts forever. Therefore he is able, once and forever, to save those who come to God through him. He lives forever to intercede with God on their behalf. He is the kind of high priest we need because he is holy and blameless, unstained by sin. He has been set apart from sinners and has been given the highest place of honor in heaven. Unlike those other high priests, he does not need to offer sacrifices every day. They did this for their own sins first and then for the sins of the people. But Jesus did this once for all when he offered himself as the sacrifice for the people's sins. The law appointed high priests who were limited by human weakness. But after the law was given, God appointed his Son with an oath, and his Son has been made the perfect High Priest forever.
>
> Hebrews 7:23-28 (NLT)

The original tabernacle structure with its holy furnishings was built after Moses received the detailed building instructions from God while on Mount Sinai in the wilderness. Later during the time of the Judges, the tabernacle would be set up in Bethel, then in Shiloh, then on to Kirjath-jearim, and eventually, when King David came on the scene, he had it taken to Zion (Mount Moriah), in Jerusalem. The humble outward tentlike structure of the tabernacle would eventually be disassembled with its curtains and boards and safely stored away. King Solomon utilized the original blueprint that God gave to

Moses and worked with his father, David, to incorporate additional insights that allowed him to construct what would become the most renowned temple that the world has ever seen. There simply wasn't, nor has there ever been any structure on the earth like it since. It had so much gold in it that it would be impossible to reconstruct something similar in the current era in which we now live. However, in the near future, Jesus will reign for one thousand years from Jerusalem as King over the whole earth. At that time, there will be a new temple built that is referenced in great detail by the prophet Ezekiel that will be the most beautiful temple structure of all time. The nations of the world will come there to worship King Jesus (Zechariah 14:16).

Eventually, the glorious temple built by Solomon would be destroyed by the invading armies of Nebuchadnezzar, but another temple that was much less grandiose was built under the leadership of Zerubbabel. In 20 BC, Herod the Great reconstructed the Temple built by Zerubbabel and its surrounding courts and buildings. Herod recruited 10,000 workmen and more than doubled the temple mount area to thirty-six acres. He built a massive retaining wall and backfilled the empty area with rock and dirt so that he could raise and level the area to give it a consistently flat surface. The Temple that Herod built is the same temple where Jesus was dedicated to God as an infant according to the Law of Moses, where He would later cast out the money changers, and where He frequently taught in the temple courts. This temple was completely destroyed by the Roman army under the leadership of Titus in AD 70.

The Jewish historian Josephus tells us that the temple built by Herod did not have the Ark of the Covenant in the Holy of Holies. There are various theories about what could have happened to the Ark of the Covenant, but it appears most likely it is hidden in a secret chamber deep within the temple mount. Rabbi Yehuda Meir Getz (1924–1995) agrees with this view. For decades he was the rabbi of the Western Wall in Jerusalem. The Western Wall tunnels were a second home for him. He spent most of his nights there and was well acquainted with the maze of tunnels beneath the temple mount and their secrets. He said the Ark of the Covenant never left Jerusalem during the Babylonian destruction but was hidden in a secret chamber beneath the temple and is still there to this day. The following verse gives insight into this school of thought.

> Then he said to the Levites who taught all Israel, who were holy to the LORD: "Put the holy ark in the house which Solomon the son of David, king of Israel, built. It shall no longer be a burden on your shoulders. Now serve the LORD your God and His people Israel."
>
> 2 Chronicles 25:3

The Hebrew word used here for "house" is *bayith*. It may also be translated as "inner chambers," "dungeon," or "nethermost point." The ark was never placed back into the temple, the house of God, but rather was moved to a hidden chamber underground. King Josiah recognized the looming threat posed by the Babylonians and Egyptians. These two empires were battling each other at the time, and Israel was caught in the middle. This is why he had the ark hidden. We do know that the golden lampstand, the table of showbread, and the altar of incense were in the Holy Place and were in usage in Herod's Temple. Because the incense was offered twice a day, it had to be prepared ahead of time. Writings from the Ashkenazi Jewish prayer book reveal how the incense was made. As you read the following description, keep in mind that a *maneh* weighed exactly one pound.

> The Rabbis taught: How was the incense compounded? Three hundred and sixty-eight manim (A maneh is a weight; plural, manim.) were comprised therein, three hundred and sixty-five corresponding to the number of days in the solar year, one maneh for each day—half in the morning and half in the afternoon. From the three remaining manim the Kohein Gadol brought two handfuls [into the Holy of Holies] on Yom Kippur; [for which purpose] they were put back into the mortar on the eve of Yom Kippur, and ground [again] very thoroughly, in order to make them very fine. Eleven kinds of spices were used for it. They were:

1) balm, 2) onycha, 3) galbanum, 4) frankincense—by weight,
seventy maneh of each; 5) myrrh, 6) cassia, 7) spikenard and 8)
saffron—in weight sixteen maneh of each; 9) twelve maneh of
costus, 10) three of aromatic bark, and 11) nine of cinnamon.
[Also used in the incense compound were:] Nine kabin (A kab
is a sixth of a se'ah.) of Carshina lye, Cyprus wine [measuring]
three s'in and three kabin—if he had no Cyprus wine, he could
use strong white wine—a fourth of a kab of Sodom salt, and a
minute quantity of maaleh ashan. (This herb causes the smoke of
the burning incense to ascend in a straight line.) Rabbi Nosson of
Babylonia says, Jordan amber was added of a minute quantity, and
if one added honey, (Included are various sweeteners such as dates
and other fruits.) it (the incense) became unfit; and if one omitted
(The same is true if one were to add to the prescribed number of
eleven spices.)—Etz Yosef any of its spices he was liable to the
death penalty."[45]

The eleven items that made up the holy incense represent the
prayer life of Jesus when He was upon the earth. We are to model our
prayer life after the Lord's example so that our prayers rise as incense
to our Father in heaven. The eleven components used in the incense
were:

1. Stacte. This is a whitish/clear-colored sap that drips from
    the tapping of balsam trees. It speaks of meekness. Quantity:
    seventy pounds.

2. Onycha. The Jewish sages primarily agree that onycha is
    a gum resin exuded by the branches of the rockrose bush.
    Onycha speaks of laying down your life for God. It represents
    being fully sold out to God. Onycha is the Greek word for
    the Hebrew word *shecheleth*. The Greek word means "nail."
    The petals on the flowers of the rockrose bush have a color of
    brilliant scarlet rose that deepens into black. There is a mark
    on each petal that resembles a human fingernail. Onycha
    is an intentional play on the word onyx which was a dark
    and black-colored gem found on the breastplate of the high

priest. After the resin from the rockrose matures, it becomes black. In preparation to be used for the holy incense, it would first be scrubbed with five gallons of *karshina* lye, a cleansing agent, in order to whiten it, and then soaked in ten gallons of *kafrisin* wine in order to intensify its fragrance. Quantity: seventy pounds.

3. Galbanum. A foul-smelling substance extracted from a certain type of wood. Without galbanum, the incense would not have had its overall beautiful fragrance. A certain chemical reaction takes place when galbanum is added that synthesizes and intensifies the overall beauty of the incense. Over the years, I have found galbanum to represent the spiritual discipline of fasting. Similar to how galbanum has a very unpleasant smell, fasting is repulsive to the carnal and soulish nature of man. Fasting is not something that is incorporated into our lives because of its beauty, but rather because it is a divine method of generating spiritual power when it is coupled with prayer. While quite a few modern-day preachers dismiss fasting as being out of date and irrelevant, the truth is that Jesus included it as being one of the three core disciplines that He instructed all of His disciples to practice regularly (Matthew 6:1-4, 5-7, 16-18). Galbanum was a critical ingredient of the holy incense. Without galbanum, the incense would not have had its mystifying beauty that made it smell so otherworldly. Without fasting joined with prayer, there are certain blessings from the Lord that will constantly elude you, causing the impossible to never seem possible. Make sure that you include galbanum (a symbol of fasting) in your incense (a symbol of prayer) in your devotion to the Lord. Quantity: seventy pounds.

4. Frankincense. A resinous substance derived from the sap of certain trees. Frankincense speaks of faith. All of our prayers must be prayed in faith, without doubting, in order to be effective. Quantity: seventy pounds.

5. Myrrh. A gum resin extracted from a certain type of tree. Like stacte, it also speaks of meekness. So we see that the holy incense contained a double dose of meekness. May we give special attention to this area of our lives as well. Quantity: sixteen pounds.

6. Cassia. A cinnamon-like bark that has beautiful purple flowers. Its smell is very similar to cloves. It appears to have been in great demand in ancient times as a luxury item. Cassia represents the royalty of the believer. It was also the name of Job's second daughter, Keziah (Job 42:14). Quantity: sixteen pounds.

7. Spike Lavender. An herb. It represents purity. This is important to understand as the Holy Spirit desires to take us into visions and revelations of Christ, for the pure in heart will see God. Quantity: sixteen pounds.

8. Saffron. A spice. It speaks of giving God your best effort. There are some offerings that the Lord refuses to receive (Malachi 1:8). We must never offer God second best but be willing to release our best. Saffron comes from the three bright, thin stalks that grow from the crocus flower. It is mentioned by King Solomon:

Your plants are an orchard of pomegranates

With pleasant fruits,

Fragrant henna with spikenard,

Spikenard and saffron,

Calamus and cinnamon,

With all trees of frankincense,

Myrrh and aloes,

With all the chief spices.

Song of Solomon 4:13-14

It takes over 4,000 crocus flowers to produce a single ounce of dried saffron spice. Saffron is still considered the most expensive spice in the world. At the time of this writing, one pound of saffron cost over $5,000. Quantity: a staggering sixteen pounds.

9. Costus. An herb whose leaves are shaped like that of an arrowhead. Quantity: twelve pounds.

10. Aromatic bark. The bark of the cinnamon tree. Quantity: three pounds.

11. Cinnamon. A spice that comes from the bark of the camphor tree that has been dried. Quantity: nine pounds.

In addition to these eleven ingredients, the following were also part of the incense.

12. Salt of Sodom. A fine-grained salt from the Dead Sea. Quantity: one-eighth of a gallon.

13. Jordan amber. A plant that grows on the banks of the Jordan River. Quantity: a minute amount.

14. Maaleh Ashan. Last but certainly not least, a secret substance that caused the smoke to rise straight up. Quantity: a very small amount.[46]

During the days of King David, the priests had become so numerous that they were divided into twenty-four groups that were appointed to each serve once a week at the tabernacle, from Sabbath to Sabbath. According to the Talmud, in the timeframe in which Jesus ministered, there were 24,000 priests that lived in Jerusalem. There were thousands of other priests who lived in designated priestly towns in the countryside. On a normal day at the temple, there would be one thousand priests who were present, along with a larger number of Levites. During the great festivals such as Passover, Pentecost, and Tabernacles, the Jewish historian Josephus said there would be over two million Jewish pilgrims who would come to Jerusalem to celebrate and worship. On one particular Passover, we are told by Josephus that there were 2.7 million pilgrims who came up to Jerusalem. He was an eyewitness to this event as well as being from a priestly family himself, although we don't know if he ever served at the Temple. The number of livestock that would have accompanied these pilgrims to be given for sacrifice would have been enormous. This required that the majority of the priests from throughout Israel would all be gathered in Jerusalem to serve in well-organized rotations at the Temple during the three major festivals.

The priests who were chosen to serve in the Temple in the Holy Place were selected by the drawing of lots. Only the high priests could go into the Holy Of Holies, but regular priests served in the Holy Place. Lots were drawn to determine what priests would serve in a particular assignment. The drawing of lots was established after an unfortunate incident occurred when two priests were running to see who could get to the brazen altar first to remove the ashes. While running up the ramp, one priest pushed the other, causing him to fall and break his arm. This accident carried serious repercussions because it meant that the injured priest could never serve in the temple service again because now he had a permanent defect, as mentioned in the following scriptures.

> And the Lord spoke to Moses, saying, "Speak to Aaron, saying: 'No man of your descendants in succeeding generations, who has any defect, may approach to offer the bread of his God. For any man who has a defect shall not approach: a man blind or lame, who has a marred face or any limb too long, a man who has a broken foot or broken hand.'"
>
> Leviticus 21:16-19

The priest with the broken arm could no longer eat from the meats that the priests received in the offerings. He also had a great desire taken away from him because he could never approach the holy sanctuary. A method of receiving special offerings was established in the temple to financially support those priests who were cut off from temple service. The priestly family of Din decided that from then on, lots would be drawn to guard the earnestness of the priests who sought to serve in ways that displayed their zeal and loyalty to the temple of God. Choosing by lot also prevented favoritism from being a factor in the selection.

For the regular priests, it was a tremendous honor and a rarity to be chosen to serve in the Temple. Because there were thousands of priests, a priest was only allowed once in his lifetime to burn the holy incense in the Holy Place. The system of drawing lots determined who would officiate at the altar of incense. Out of all the temple activities, this was considered to be the most desirable act of worship for a priest, and they were only allowed to do it once because there was a special blessing associated with burning the incense on the golden altar. For a priest to be chosen to do this would be considered the greatest day of his life.

Each morning, one of the appointed priestly officers would make an announcement in the courtyard of the Temple calling for all of the priests who had never offered incense before to come near to him. In the time of Herod's Temple, the priests would then go to the Hall of Hewn Stones and draw lots to determine which individual priest would perform the incense offering. A priest was only allowed to do this once because the fifteen older priestly officers who oversaw the temple activities wanted as many priests as possible to experience this blessing. What was the special blessing associated with performing the burning of incense? The answer is that God would release a blessing of financial wealth upon the priest who performed this sacrifice. The rabbis verified this blessing through the following scripture:

They shall teach Jacob Your judgments,

And Israel Your law.

They shall put incense before You,

And a whole burnt sacrifice on Your altar.

Bless his substance, Lord,

And accept the work of his hands;

Strike the loins of those who rise against him,
And of those who hate him, that they rise not again.

Deuteronomy 33:10-11

According to Nachmanides (a leading medieval Jewish scholar, 1194–1270), this is a plea by Moses for God to "bless his substance" by granting the tribe of Levi wealth and plenty of financial resources so that they can study Torah. By being able to devote their time and full mental energies to studying Torah and not needing to be concerned about having enough money, the priests would be well versed in the law. This level of expertise would therefore prevent them from making mistakes that would endanger Israelite lives or even their own lives. God gave very precise instructions to Moses concerning His laws. The priests had to know the law extremely well in order to keep it and to accurately teach the people, and this required diligent study and training. Each priest understood that the blessing of their substance by the Lord during the incense offering was considered a blessing of financial wealth that would endure in his lifetime and throughout eternity. This is very important for a congregation to understand concerning their pastor. The man or woman who is called by God full-time into the ministry should never be distracted from their ministry work of prayer and Bible study because of personal lack. It bestows blessing and dignity upon a church congregation when they tangibly display their love and financial support for their pastor and his family. This includes an allowance for a good salary that sees that his or her essential needs of food, clothing, housing, transportation, and extra for savings and other needs are comfortably supplied.

Only wood from the fig tree was used on the altar of incense because the rabbis said it made the best charcoal to burn incense upon. While the lamb was being slain in the sacrifice outside of the sanctuary, one priest would gather up some coals from the brazen altar, which was located in the outer court. These coals were placed in a golden vessel and then taken inside the Holy Place. The priest who would actually ignite the incense on the altar acquired the portion of incense that was to be used and entered the Holy Place with two other priests. The two priests removed all the instruments used to clean the golden lampstand. One of them would also have spread the hot coals on the altar of incense, but he would not place the incense on it. At this point, everyone left except for the priest, who was to ignite the incense. In the outer court area, the chief priest on duty would announce, "The time of incense had come."[47] At this point, all the Jews would prostrate themselves in silent prayer while the incense was lit. This would have been within the time frame when Zacharias saw the angel Gabriel in a vision, as Luke records in his Gospel.

> So it was, that while he was serving as priest before God in the order of his division, according to the custom of the priesthood, his lot fell to burn incense when he went into the temple of the Lord. And the whole multitude of the people was praying outside at the hour of incense. Then an angel of the Lord appeared to him, standing on the right side of the altar of incense.
>
> Luke 1:8-11

When the priest emerged from the Holy Place, he would be joined by the other priests who assisted him. He would then lead the people and his fellow priests in the following blessing:

The Lord bless you and keep you;

The Lord make His face shine upon you,

And be gracious to you;

The Lord lift up His countenance upon you,

And give you peace.

Numbers 6:24-26

This would also explain why the Jews were so amazed at Zacharias's inability to speak because it was customary for the priest who performed the incense offering to pronounce the blessing over the people, yet he was unable to say a single word.

"But when he came out, he could not speak to them; and they perceived that he had seen a vision in the temple, for he beckoned to them and remained speechless" (Luke 1:22).

In order for the priests to offer the holy incense as a sacrifice, the incense had to first be produced. The priestly family responsible for creating the incense was the house of Avtinas. The formula for preparing incense for the Temple was a closely guarded secret held by this family of the Second Temple period when the Herodians ruled Israel. No one, not even the other priestly families, knew the identity of the secret ingredient of the incense called *maaleh ashan* except members of the priestly family of the House of Avtinas. It was necessary for maaleh ashan to be placed in the incense even though it did not have any fragrance. If maaleh ashan was not added to the mixture, the incense would burn, but there would not be a thick and heavy ascending smoke. The Torah speaks of a "cloud" of smoke, and the only substance that made this heavy smoke is the maaleh ashan. If a different type of herb was used, the smoke would not go directly up, but it would spread out to all sides when used in the Holy of Holies. It would then not be right over the ark cover, and the Torah says explicitly, "The cloud of incense shall cover the ark cover" (Leviticus 16:13).

Twice daily, the priests offered the incense in the Holy Place. But once a year, on the day of atonement, the high priest would take coals from the altar and place them in a censer. He would then take two handfuls of incense and pass beyond the veil into the Holy of Holies. There, he would place the incense upon the coals and let it smoke before the Lord. Rabbis taught that this cloud of smoke must conceal the ark cover so that the high priest did not see the divine presence between the cherubim.

The house of Avtinas took great efforts to honor the temple of God through the role they held as the incense makers. For example, the men of the Avtinas family never allowed their wives to walk outside of their homes perfumed. If a man from the house of Avtinas married a woman from another house, then it was on the condition that she would not wear perfume. They took these precautionary measures so that people wouldn't say they used the holy incense to perfume themselves. It was in their hearts to be above reproach and to fulfill the following scripture: "Then afterward you may return and be blameless before the LORD and before Israel" (Numbers 32:22b).

Despite the pure motives of the house of Avtinas, the rabbis were upset that this family did not wish to teach the other priests how to prepare the incense. When pressed to explain their position, they responded that their family tradition included a firm belief that one day the Temple was destined to be destroyed. They logically reasoned that if the incense formula were known and the Temple were destroyed, then an unworthy person could create the incense and use it in the worship of idols. Their explanation didn't go over very well with the Temple authorities. The insistence of the Avtinas family to guard their secret formula of the incense so angered the rabbis that they fired them and ordered them to leave the Temple.

Turning to another option, the Temple authorities sent for Jewish experts from Alexandria, Egypt, with the hope that they might duplicate the procedure of making the holy incense. The Jewish perfume compounders (who were modern-day chemists) from Alexandria were brought in, and they did succeed in compounding the incense, but they couldn't figure out the special way in which the Avtinas family caused the smoke to rise. It is said that the secret ingredient known only to this family possibly came from the stem of the date tree, which causes the smoke to go up perfectly and then, at a certain point, descend and spread out properly. Eventually, the rabbis sent for the Avtinas family to return to their former job. However, they refused to come until it was agreed that their former wages would be doubled. The Temple authorities agreed to do so and came to the realization of a spiritual rule that they saw at work in which "one man cannot touch that which is designated for another."[48]

In my life and ministry, I have seen this same principle play out at various times. Once when I was at my office, I received a phone call from one of my church members asking if he and his wife could stop by to ask my counsel on a certain matter. I invited them to come over, and they soon arrived. As they sat down, they wasted no time in getting to the point. The man said, "Pastor Steven, my wife and I are in a disagreement over the giving of an offering. We want to give an offering, but we can't agree on the amount." I asked a few questions and was surprised to find out that the offering they felt led to give was not for my ministry but rather for another man's ministry. I personally felt their request for insight, in this case, was a little bit odd, perhaps insensitive; however, I did happen to know the minister they were referring to. He was a good minister who was doing good work for the Lord in a different country. Even though the offering wasn't going to be for my ministry, I still endeavored to offer counsel that would be in agreement with the will of God. Both the husband and wife had PhDs from major universities. They were both very intelligent, and the wife attended our own church prayer gatherings from time to time. However, he was intellectually dominant and did not have an established prayer life like she did. Because of this, his spirit was not developed to a degree where he could clearly discern the leading of the Holy Spirit. Looking at him, I said, "How much do you sense the Lord wants this offering to be?" He replied, "Five thousand dollars." Next, I looked at her and said, "How much do you sense the offering is to be?" She calmly responded, "One hundred thousand dollars." Through a strong inward witness of the Holy Spirit, I knew that she was correct. I sat there quietly for about two or three seconds and realized I could potentially tip their decision in the wrong direction if I chose to be envious of another man's blessing. I could have said, "You should only give $5,000." But I knew the right thing to do was to help my fellow minister receive what was designated for him by the Lord. With peace in my heart, I confidently said, "The offering is supposed to be $100,000." The husband happily replied, "Well then, that is what we will do." The next day they sent the offering they had committed to give.

I had an interesting encounter with an angel one day while I was at my house. I walked from my office that was upstairs and went down to the kitchen to get a snack. It was in the afternoon, and nobody else was home. I made a sandwich and took some potato chips, and placed it all on a plate. With the plate in one hand, I grabbed a Dr. Pepper from the refrigerator with the other hand and began to walk back to my office. As I passed through the hallway leading to the stairs, I suddenly became aware of the presence of an angel standing to my right, about five feet away from me there in the hallway. Although I could not see him, his presence was undeniable. I stopped and closed my eyes, holding my food and drink in each hand. The moment I closed my eyes, the angel spoke to me and said, "There is no need for you ever to be envious of any other man's ministry. The unique and specific promises that God has given to you are more than enough to make you happy." Then, I saw a crystal clear vision of the main desire of my heart held before me. It was the thing that I most greatly desired for the Lord to do for me, and seeing it made me smile from ear to ear. I then could see the angel standing right where I had sensed him to be. I noticed that he did not have wings like some angels do. This angel exuded a very calm and peaceful demeanor. Envy is wanting something that another person possesses. While I have never struggled with the sin of envy, I have learned to guard my heart in this area because we never want to be displeased at someone else's success. Having our own personal promises from God is a major key over envy and jealousy in our lives. Our eyes must not be on what others have. Rather, we should learn to ask God for *our own* promises and focus on them, just as the house of Avtinas did.

Most ultra-Orthodox Jews believe that a future temple will be rebuilt in Jerusalem on Mount Moriah. Because of this expectation, both Orthodox Jewish scholars and Christian Zionists have a keen interest in how the holy incense was produced. This quest for knowledge regarding temple artifacts and items used in the holy incense is of great importance to any archeologist who digs in Israel. In April of 1992, Vendyl Jones, a Baptist preacher from Texas, who became an amateur archeologist, and his team of volunteers discovered 1,300 pounds of a very finely ground reddish-brown organic substance. Jones was convinced that his discovery was a stockpile of holy incense that was stored away after the destruction of the Temple in Jerusalem in AD 70. It was hidden and sealed inside a rock silo in an unexplored part of the Qumran cave complex. The Qumran cave in which it was found is referred to as the "spice cave." A coin from the third year of the First Jewish Revolt (67–68 CE) had been placed in the spices. The entrance of the cave had been sealed with a cultural dome of debris and rubble that was eleven layers thick.

Later, a detailed scientific analysis that looked at the "atomic footprint" of the substance revealed that it contained traces of at least eight of the eleven spices that were used in the making of the holy incense. The substance appears to have been some form of a premix of the holy incense that was kept for "final assembly" until the time it would be needed. Larry Borntrager was working with Vendyl Jones when the discovery was made. In an interview in 2019, he confirmed that in the cave where the stash was located, the team also found "Sodom salt from the Dead Sea, off to the side on a ledge, and other ingredients that were not mixed in until the ketoret was burned."[49]

Although Jewish law prohibits personal or ritual use of the Temple incense, a small amount was burned with hydrochloric acid and not fire. It was done under rabbinic guidance for the purpose of testing whether it was still usable after 2,000 years. The results were quite compelling and indicated that the substance could be the authentic holy incense. Although the spices had lost some of their aromatic factors over the two thousand years since their burial, they were still powerful. After the experiment was completed, the aroma lingered in the area for several days. Several scientists present reported that their hair and clothing retained the aroma.

The following account of this testing process is taken from an assessment made by Dr. Terry Hutter.

> The aroma released from the "spices" compound during its processing was profuse and almost immediate. It initially saturated my hands as well as the clothes that I was wearing. Within a matter of minutes my laboratory and the surrounding area (for

an area of several meters) was affected by the scent released from the "spices." The intensity of the odor also awakened my dog (a miniature Dachshund) who was asleep in her bed in the lab. On the first day of processing, the aroma was so intense that I could almost "taste" it [perhaps this was the original effect during Temple times]. In any case, that evening, upon my return home, the scent that had attached itself on my body and clothes was really apparent to both my wife and daughter. During the course of the week, the odor lessened slightly but was still noticeable in and around my lab. Within a few weeks the distinct aroma of the spices diminished to a "freshness or cleanness" of the air in my lab and the surrounding area. This aroma was in evidence, if even so slightly, for approximately two months. On days of high humidity the aroma would return with greater intensity.[50]

While there are many secrets that still surround the production of the holy incense, there will soon come a day in which this lost art will be revived in the new temple that will be built in Jerusalem. The rabbis have been greatly anticipating this moment when the temple services will be reinstituted and priestly functions will once again commence. On that occasion, the house of Avtinas will be reinstated to their position. Rabbi Yishmael (AD 90–135) was a descendant from a wealthy priestly family in Upper Galilee. He was an accomplished scholar who shared the following insight that took place between himself and a young child descended from the Avtinas family. This story further unveils the prophetic destiny of the house of Avtinas.

Rabbi Akiva said: One time Rabbi Yishmael ben Loga related to me: One time I and one of the descendants of the House of Avtinas went out to the field to collect herbs, and I saw that he laughed and he cried. I said to him: Why did you cry? He said to me: I was reminded of the honor of my forefathers, how important they were in the Temple. I said to him: And why did you laugh? He said to me: The Holy One, Blessed be He, is going to restore it to us in the future and we will be honored again. I said to him: And why are you reminded of this now? He said to me: The smoke-raising herb is before me, here in the field, reminding me of the past. I said to him: Show it to me; which one is it? He said to me: We are bound by oath not to show it to any person other than the members of our family.[51]

Upon Mount Moriah, there have been three temples that have been built and dedicated to the Lord, which are the temples of Solomon, Zerubbabel, and Herod. Two further temples are yet to be built. The next temple to be constructed will again be built by the Jews and dedicated to God, but it is destined to be known as the temple invaded by the Antichrist. Jesus is the Messiah and has already come. Because many of the Jews have rejected the true Messiah, they will be duped into receiving a false Christ. This false Christ is actually an agent of Satan, who will eventually set up an image in the Holy Place and will demand the world to worship him. Jesus spoke of the abomination that makes desolate standing in the holy place.

> "Therefore when you see the 'abomination of desolation,' spoken of by Daniel the prophet, standing in the holy place" (whoever reads, let him understand), "then let those who are in Judea flee to the mountains. Let him who is on the housetop not go down to take anything out of his house."
>
> Matthew 24:15-17

No other place on earth is identified by the Jews as the Holy Place, except the Temple Mount in Jerusalem. Jesus was declaring, in effect, that the temple would be rebuilt. In 167 BC, a Greek ruler by the name of Antiochus Epiphanies sacrificed a pig on the altar in the Temple in Jerusalem and forced the priests to eat its flesh. He then set up in the Temple an idol of Zeus, the pagan deity he believed himself to be, and demanded that the idol be worshipped. This event was a precursor to the abomination of desolation that is yet to come. Antiochus never did confirm a covenant with Israel for seven years, so the prophecies of Daniel were speaking towards the end of the age when the Antichrist will come on the scene. This proves that the temple will be rebuilt because Israel will only return to animal sacrifices that are performed upon an altar on Mount Moriah on the authentic temple site. In order to do this, they must have a temple that brings legitimacy to those sacrifices in accordance with the Mosaic Law and its guidelines.

> The ruler will make a treaty with the people for a period of one set of seven, but after half this time, he will put an end to the sacrifices and offerings. And as a climax to all his terrible deeds, he will set up a sacrilegious object that causes desecration, until the fate decreed for this defiler is finally poured out on him.
>
> Daniel 9:27 (NLT)

The Antichrist will establish a covenant with Israel for seven years and then break it halfway through. The abomination of desolation will be some form of an image of the Antichrist that appears to be alive, being able to speak and communicate, perhaps through some type of AI (Artificial Intelligence). The false prophet will position this image of the Antichrist to stand in the Holy Place. Within this time frame, the Antichrist will proclaim himself to be God and will forcefully demand all to worship him. This predetermined event releases three-and-a-half years of great tribulation upon the earth that will begin to unfold immediately. Apostle Paul wrote much concerning the reign of the Antichrist and the temple that must be built in Jerusalem.

> Let no one deceive you in any way. For that day will not come, unless the rebellion comes first, and the man of lawlessness is revealed, the son of destruction, who opposes and exalts himself against every so-called god or object of worship, so that he takes his seat in the temple of God, proclaiming himself to be God.
>
> 2 Thessalonians 2:3-4 (ESV)

We see that Paul clearly states that the Antichrist will sit in the temple dedicated to God that has been constructed by the Jews. It is not a temple that the Antichrist himself shall build, but its construction will have been completed and made ready by the Jews for the coming Messiah. However, we know that Messiah Jesus has already come, and most of the Jewish religious leaders of His day did not receive Him. The Antichrist will come as an imposter and as a fraud and will deceive many of the Jews through his trickery.

"I have come in my Father's name, and you do not receive me. If another comes in his own name, you will receive him" (John 5:43).

Before the Antichrist comes, the temple must be rebuilt, and the functions of the temple must be operative, and this would include the two daily incense offerings made at the altar of incense in the Holy Place. The ultra-Orthodox Jews in Jerusalem now have the plans drawn out for the new temple, and the construction of all of the furnishings have already been completed, including the golden lampstand, the table of showbread, the altar of incense, the clothing for the priests, the clothing and golden miter for the high priest along with many other necessary details.

> And I was given a measuring rod like a staff, and I was told, "Get up and measure the Temple of God, and the altar, and count those who worship there. But leave out of your measurement the courtyard outside the Temple—do not measure that at all. For it has been given over to the nations, and they will trample over the holy city for forty-two months."
>
> Revelation 11:1-2 (Phillips)

The temple that Apostle John was instructed to measure could not have been a heavenly temple since the gentiles will not have the ability to tread underfoot that which is in heaven. At the writing of this vision, there was no longer a temple that existed in Jerusalem. The former temple that stood during the Lord's time had been destroyed in AD 70 by Titus and the Roman legions. John was given this vision during the time of Emperor Domitian, which was circa AD 90. What John saw in his vision was the temple spoken of by Daniel, Jesus, and Paul that is yet to be built in Jerusalem in the last days. It is critical that we understand that when we see the Jews building a new temple upon the Temple Mount, we can know with utmost certainty that the end is very near.

Eventually, there will be the building of the Millennial Temple, as described in rich detail by the prophet Ezekiel. In a vision, Ezekiel saw the future temple that will one day stand in Jerusalem. There has never been a temple built in Israel that has the same measurements that Ezekiel was shown; therefore, we can be certain that this temple will be built in the days ahead of us. This will take place during the thousand-year reign of Jesus as King over the whole earth as He governs from Jerusalem. His reign will commence when His feet stand upon the Mount of Olives. In this temple, the Lord Jesus will be visibly present and will be worshipped. When we study the scriptures concerning Ezekiel's Temple, we see that missing from the temple are the Ark of the Covenant, the golden lampstand, and the altar of incense. This can be explained by the fact that the Lord Himself will be there (the Ark), and He is the Light (menorah) and the Fragrance of Heaven (altar of incense) in this temple.

Although the church age will have been completed by this time, we who are believers in Christ will be able to journey from heaven to earth to enjoy viewing the various kingdom activities in Jerusalem. Some redeemed saints will be qualified to rule and reign with the Lord on the earth. The life that we live now is so important because it affects our eternal ministry. This is addressed in the book of Ezekiel, chapter forty-four, which emphasizes how we must strive to obey the laws of God and not follow the fleshly wishes of the people.

> And the men of the tribe of Levi who abandoned me when Israel strayed away from me to worship idols must bear the consequences of their unfaithfulness. They may still be Temple guards and gatekeepers, and they may slaughter the animals brought for burnt offerings and be present to help the people. But they encouraged my people to worship idols, causing Israel to fall into deep sin. So I have taken a solemn oath that they must bear the consequences for their sins, says the Sovereign LORD. They may not approach me to minister as priests. They may not touch any of my holy things or the holy offerings, for they must bear the shame of all the detestable sins they have committed. They are to serve as the

Temple caretakers, taking charge of the maintenance work and performing general duties.

Ezekiel 44:10-14 (NLT)

In the days of David, there were two principal priests, Zadok and Abiathar. Zadok proved faithful to Solomon when Solomon rose to the throne. But Abiathar followed Adonijah when Adonijah attempted to take the throne through conspiracy. Zadok followed God's choice while Abiathar followed the wishes of the people. Abiathar's error proved very costly.

"So Solomon removed Abiathar from the priesthood of the LORD, fulfilling the word the LORD had spoken at Shiloh about the house of Eli" (1 Kings 2:27, NIV).

Abiathar was a descendant of the unfaithful High Priest Eli. Eli became an infamous example of someone who honored his reprobate sons more than he did the Lord. Limitations are placed on the unfaithful in their eternal ministry. However, rewards are promised to those who are faithful to their current ministry.

> However, the Levitical priests of the family of Zadok continued to minister faithfully in the Temple when Israel abandoned me for idols. These men will serve as my ministers. They will stand in my presence and offer the fat and blood of the sacrifices, says the Sovereign LORD. They alone will enter my sanctuary and approach my table to serve me. They will fulfill all my requirements.

Ezekiel 44:15-16 (NLT)

A strong prayer life positions you to stay faithful like Zadok, the priest. In return for this loyalty, there is granted an unusual nearness to the Lord Himself. Even when the great falling away takes place (2 Thessalonians 2:3), you will remain steadfast in Christ. Therefore, keep moving forward on the designated path of holiness, obedience, and blessing that God has for you. Stay in your lane and focus on the specific promises that God has made to you. Like the house of Avtinas, we each have our specialty. May you rise to the very top in your field of expertise, and may your prayers rise like incense before the Lord, just as the holy incense did in the daily sacrifices at the temple.

Creating Your Own Spiritual Fragrance

Faith to receive a specific blessing of God comes from hearing what the Word of God says about that particular subject and then acting upon what you have heard with a receptive heart. The Word of God establishes a firm platform that we can stand on and confidently expect that what God did for others, He can do for us as well. We have seen various scriptures that reveal the examples of supernatural fragrance, and this builds faith in our hearts to receive and enjoy the same blessing. Throughout the pages of this book, we have also seen past and modern-day examples of Christians from different times in church history who have also demonstrated this gift. Their testimonies are living proof that God still desires to display His glory through the miraculous sign and wonder of supernatural fragrances. If you have a desire to experience this same gift in your own life, then I want to pray for you at the conclusion of this chapter. By exercising your faith and walking close to God, you, too, will have testimonies to share concerning how God has opened up the prophetic realm of heavenly fragrance to you.

Everything in life has a price tag. Someone once said that salvation is free, and it doesn't cost anything. While this is technically true, it does not, however, convey a deeper truth that is important for us to understand. Salvation is free for anyone who is willing to receive Christ Jesus into their heart through faith. The reason salvation is free is because Jesus paid the full price for our sins while on the cross at Calvary. Salvation was beyond our ability to pay, so Jesus paid it for us by sacrificing His life for us. Jesus is the ransom payment for our sins. A *ransom* is money paid to rescue someone from captivity. Jesus died and shed His blood to ransom us from the condemnation and captivity of sin. While salvation is free for anyone to receive, it cost Jesus His life. So there is a price tag of some type associated with anything that we desire, even if we didn't directly pay for it ourselves.

What is the price tag for experiencing supernatural fragrances? We know that all of the gifts of the Holy Spirit are technically grace gifts. In other words, *you can't earn them* because they are distributed to each one in the church by the Holy Spirit as the Spirit wills. Yet, at the same time, we are also told by Apostle Paul that we are to *eagerly desire* gifts of the Spirit (1 Corinthians 14:1). Our desire has a lot to do with what is given to us by the Spirit. Desire can be fueled by a special ingredient (the price tag) that is often overlooked in the recipe of faith. There are two primary price tags that surround supernatural fragrances. One of them is known simply as *exposure*.

I define *exposure* as being a personal awareness of how God is blessing other Christians in a particular way and realizing that if God is doing it for them, then He can do it for me too. Exposure includes a basic understanding of how someone you emulate lived their life and what they chose to put their focus on. This works on a personal level as well as for a collective group of believers. Many revivals springboard off another revival. The Azusa Street Revival was fueled by those who traveled from Europe to America and gave eyewitness accounts (exposure) and testimonies of salvation, healings, and miracles (more exposure) about the Welsh revival. What does this positive type of exposure do for those who hear it with an open heart? It creates an inward illumination that says, "Well, if they can have it, then so can we."

My wife and I live in a beautiful but rural area of North Carolina. Just a few days ago, we met a young person in their twenties who has never left the local county in which we live. I'm not speaking of someone who has never left the state, I'm referring only to the county. This is certainly not the only adult I've met who has never ventured beyond the county line. I once met a woman in her late thirties who had never driven beyond the county line. You may think, *How can that be possible in this modern day?* Well, I'll assure you it is a definite reality for some people here. Limited exposure can make a person mistakenly think that the struggles and lack of opportunity they experience are the same type of life that everyone else is facing. Lack of exposure can cause a person to form mindsets that are based on myths and inaccuracies. I often tell people in my community that I lead tours to Israel, and I invite them to go with me and visit the land of Israel. In response, some look at me with much fear and trepidation and say, "Oh, but isn't it so dangerous? Aren't you afraid you'll die?" The reality is that of all the countries that I have visited, I always feel safest in Israel. Their security levels are second to none, I know this because I have been there numerous times (exposure), and I plan on going back again and again.

Countless believers in Jesus sit in churches unaware of the vast spiritual inheritance that rightfully belongs to them. This book was written about supernatural fragrances with an assurance from the Lord that if His people are exposed to this truth, then it will birth a desire in many, and they will step into the realm of prophetic smell. This is why I included the various stories about the saints: to stimulate your faith to experience the same blessing. All of the promises of God are accessed through faith. Exposure toward faith in God, to live in the miraculous is a key ingredient in experiencing the realm of supernatural fragrance. There is another hidden key that is often overlooked when it comes to not only smelling supernatural fragrances but, more importantly, emitting the fragrance of Christ. This key is the second price tag that any believer must be willing to pay in order to not only experience supernatural fragrances but also to emit them. Before I share this second price tag with you, let me briefly cover some important church history to set the context to discovering a key to Christlike fragrance.

In AD 35, the early church came under severe persecution from the Jewish religious leaders and authorities, after the martyrdom of Stephen. Many Christians moved away from Jerusalem to escape to areas that were beyond the boundaries of where the persecution was centered at. But because the gospel message is so transformative, any place where it begins to take root and bring forth fruit also causes a major shift in the way society is conducted. As the gospel spread outward in all directions, many were saved, but new persecution also began to arise from those who rejected the gospel and clung to their pagan beliefs.

In AD 64, Emperor Nero of Rome launched a tremendous wave of persecution against the Christians, burning many of them alive on stakes. The persecution escalated in AD 80 when Emperor Domitian initiated emperor worship throughout the Roman Empire, requiring everyone to worship and acknowledge him as "god the lord." The number of Christian martyrs rose as the years and several centuries slowly rolled by; wave after wave of barbaric torture, brutality, and loss of all possessions was the norm for many believers, leading to AD 303 when what is known as the Great Persecution began; an all-out attempt to extinguish Christianity. Four edicts were given by Emperor Diocletian in which (a) all church buildings were to be destroyed, (b) all biblical writings and related Christian written material were to be burned, (c) Christians were not allowed any civil rights and were considered as outlaws, and (d) all Christian ministers were ordered to be imprisoned and required to sacrifice to Roman gods.[52] The Roman Empire's wave of persecution finally drew to a halt when Constantin became the sole Roman emperor in AD 324, as Christianity then became the legal religion of the Roman Empire.

As an example of the persecution that these early Christians endured, let's briefly look at the lives of four famous martyrs whose names are Maturus, Sanctus, Blandina, and Attalus. Their martyrdom took place in the year 177 in Gaul (modern-day France) in the city of Lyons. Eusebius was a Christian historian who lived in the third century. In book five of his *Ecclesiastical History*, he records a letter sent from the Christians in Gaul (France) to their brothers in Asia (modern-day Turkey). Eusebius tells us that this letter is "worthy of perpetual memory." Here are some excerpts from that letter that inform us of these four famous martyrs:

> Blandina was filled with such power, that those who tortured her one after the other in every way from morning till evening were wearied and tired. They admitted they were baffled. They had no other torture they could apply to her. They were astonished that she remained alive. Her whole body was torn and opened up. They said that even one of the forms of torture employed was enough to have destroyed her life, not to mention so many excruciating punishments. But the blessed woman, like a noble athlete, renewed

her strength in her confession. Her declaration, "I am a Christian, and there is no evil done amongst us," brought her refreshment, rest, and insensibility to all the sufferings inflicted on her.[53]

But Sanctus also endured marvelously and superhumanly all the outrages which he suffered. While the wicked men hoped, by the continuance and severity of his tortures to wring something from him which he ought not to say, he girded himself against them with such firmness that he would not even tell his name, or the nation or city to which he belonged, or whether he was bond or free, but answered in the Roman tongue to all their questions, "I am a Christian." He confessed this instead of name and city and race and everything besides, and the people heard no other word from him. For this reason the governor and his tormentors desired to conquer him, but having nothing more that they could do to him, they finally fastened red-hot brazen plates to the most tender parts of his body. And these indeed were burned, but he continued unbending and unyielding, firm in his confession, and refreshed and strengthened by the heavenly fountain of the water of life, flowing from Christ Himself.

Sanctus' body was a witness of his sufferings, being one complete wound and bruise, pulled out of shape, and altogether unlike a human form. Christ manifested His glory, suffering in him, delivering him from his adversary, and making him an example for the others. He showed in Sanctus that nothing is fearful where the love of the Father is, and nothing painful where there is the glory of Christ. For when the wicked men tortured him a second time after some days, supposing that with his body swollen and inflamed to such a degree that he could not bear the touch of a hand, if they should again apply the same instruments, they would overcome him—or at least by his death under his sufferings others would be made afraid—not only did not this occur, but, contrary to all anyone could have expected, his body arose and stood erect in the midst of the subsequent torments, and resumed its original appearance and the use of its limbs, so that through the grace of Christ these second sufferings became to him, not torture, but healing.

[...] After these things, finally, their martyrdom was finally distributed into various kinds. [...] Therefore Maturus, Sanctus, Blandina and Attalus were led to the amphitheater to be exposed to the wild beasts, and to give to the heathen public a spectacle of cruelty, a day for fighting with wild beasts being specially appointed on account of our people.[54]

It is here that this ancient letter tells us that when these four Christians were brought into the amphitheater that a supernatural fragrance rested heavily upon them, it was said: "They were perfumed with the fragrance of Christ, so that some even thought that they were anointed with earthly perfume."[55]

Both Maturus and Sanctus passed again through every torment in the amphitheater, as if they had suffered nothing before, or rather, as if, having already conquered their antagonist in many contests, they were now striving for the crown itself. They endured again the customary running of the gauntlet and the violence of the wild beasts, and everything which the furious people called for or desired, and at last, the iron chair in which their bodies being roasted, tormented them with the fumes. And the persecutors did not stop, but were yet more enraged against them, determined to overcome their patience. But even so they did not hear a word from Sanctus except the confession which he had uttered from the beginning. So these, after their life had continued for a long time through the great conflict, were at last sacrificed, having been made a spectacle to the world throughout that day, in place of the usual variety of combats.

Blandina was suspended on a stake, and exposed to be devoured by the wild beasts who should attack her. And because she appeared as if hanging on a cross, and because of her earnest prayers, she inspired the combatants with great zeal. For they looked on her in her conflict, and beheld with their outward eyes, in the form of their sister, Him who was crucified for them, that He might persuade those who believe on Him, that everyone who suffers for the glory of Christ has fellowship always with the living God. As none of the wild beasts at that time touched her, she was taken down from the stake, and cast again into prison. She was preserved thus for another contest, so that, being victorious in more conflicts, she might make the punishment of the crooked serpent irrevocable; and, though small and weak and despised, yet being clothed with Christ the mighty and conquering Athlete, she might arouse the zeal of the brethren, and, having overcome the adversary many times, might receive through her conflict the incorruptible crown.[56]

Attalus also was loudly called for by the mob because he was a person of distinction. He entered the contests readily on account of his good conscience. He had been truly practiced in the Christian discipline and had always been a Witness of the truth among us. He was led round the amphitheater, a tablet going before him, on which was written in Latin, "This is Attalus the Christian;" The people were filled with indignation against him. But the governor, learning that he was a Roman, ordered him to be taken back to prison and kept with the rest who were there. He [the governor] had written to the Caesar about these and was waiting for his answer.[57]

Caesar was quick to answer with orders to have Attalus put to death.

For to please the people, the governor had ordered Attalus again to the wild beasts. [...] When Attalus was placed in the iron seat, and the fumes arose from his burning body, he said to the people in the Roman language: "Look! What you are doing is devouring men; but we do not devour men, nor do any other wicked thing." [One of the false charges often told against the early Christians was that they were cannibals.] And being asked, what name God has, he replied, "God does not have a name as man has."

After all these, on the last day of the contests, Blandina was again brought in, with Ponticus, a boy about fifteen years old. [Blandina was the last of the four famous martyrs to be killed. The other three finally had their throats cut after having endured every form of cruelty.] They had been brought every day to witness the sufferings of the others, and had been pressured to swear by the idols. But because they remained steadfast and despised them, the multitude became furious, so that they had no compassion for the youth of the boy nor respect for the sex of the woman. Therefore they exposed them to all the terrible sufferings and took them through the entire round of torture, repeatedly urging them to swear, but being unable to effect this; for Ponticus, encouraged by his sister so that even the heathen could see that she was confirming and strengthening him, having nobly endured every torture, gave up his spirit.

But the blessed Blandina, last of all, having, as a noble mother, encouraged her children and sent them before her victorious to the King, endured herself all their conflicts and hastened after them, glad and rejoicing in her departure as if called to a marriage supper, rather than cast to wild beasts. And, after the scourging, after the wild beasts, after the roasting seat, she was finally enclosed in a net and thrown before a bull. And having been tossed about by the animal, but feeling none of the things which were happening to her, on account of her hope and firm hold upon what had been entrusted to her, and her communion with Christ, she also was sacrificed. And the heathen themselves confessed that never among them had a woman endured so many and such terrible tortures.

But not even thus was their madness and cruelty toward the saints satisfied. For incited by the Wild Beast, wild and barbarous tribes were not easily appeased, and their violence found another peculiar opportunity in the dead bodies. For, through their lack of human reason, the fact that they had been conquered did not put them to shame, but rather further kindled their wrath like that of a wild beast, and aroused the hatred of both the governor and the people to treat us unjustly. This was in fulfillment of the Scripture: "He that is lawless, let him be lawless still, and he that is righteous, let him be righteous still."[58]

They carefully watched them day and night, so that none of them should be buried by us. They then laid out the bodies of the others—the mangled remains left by the wild beasts, the scorched remains left by the fire, and the heads of the rest along with their trunks, and for many days they had military guards see to it that we did not bury them. There were some who raged and gnashed their teeth at them, seeking to get from them further vengeance. Others laughed and mocked them, at the same time magnifying their own idols, and attributing to them the punishment inflicted on the Christians. Even the more reasonable and those somewhat sympathetic frequently reproached them saying, "Where now is their God? What good have they got from that religion which they chose in preference to their life?" Their conduct toward us was indeed confused! But our state was one of deep sorrow that we could not bury the bodies. For night did not help us in this matter; money failed to persuade; and entreaty did not move them to compassion. But they kept up the guard in every way, as if they were to gain some great advantage from the bodies of the Christians not receiving burial. The bodies of the Witnesses, after having been maltreated in every way and exposed in the open air for six days were burned. Their ashes were swept by the wicked into the river Rhone, which flows past so that no trace of them might be visible on earth. They did all this as if they had been able to overcome God. They thought they could deprive them of their second birth in order, as they said, that "they may not have hope in a resurrection. Through the Christians' trust in the resurrection they bring to us this foreign and new religion. They despise dangers and are ready to even go to death with joy. Now let us see if they will rise again, and if their God can help them and rescue them out of our hands."[59]

The emphasis on much of the early church within its first 300 years of growth was facing the potential reality of martyrdom. The willingness to die for your faith was something you had to seriously consider when accepting Christ as your Lord and Savior. Martyrdom for your faith was a real possibility that could be very well called upon and often was. The fragrance of Christ was a common manifestation resting profusely upon the Christians who refused to compromise their faith while being martyred. The recorded story of a beautiful supernatural fragrance accompanying Maturus, Sanctus, Blandina, and Attalus as they were marched into the amphitheater to die is one of many such instances associated with heavenly fragrance and Christian martyrdom. It could truly be said of them, "They did not love their lives to the death" (Revelation 12:11).

With the collapse of the Roman Empire, the overshadowing threat of martyrdom was greatly diminished. Some Christians in certain Roman provinces had become so accustomed to persecution that when the laws were changed by Constantin, it left them in somewhat of a quandary. They had become so used to living with an expectation of immediate death that they decided to look for new ways to prove to the unsaved their intense loyalty to Jesus and to demonstrate their desire to be disconnected from the world. This gave birth to what became known as the Desert Fathers. With no Roman officials seeking to chop their head off or feed them to the lions, some notable Christian leaders moved into previously uninhabitable desert areas of northern Egypt and southern Israel in an effort to live as hermits and simulate the stress, discomfort, and isolation from the society they had come to know. Over a few decades, there was a shift from a focus on martyrdom to a new focus of becoming a mature saint, willing to lay down your life and die daily by crucifying the self-nature.

The Desert Fathers taught that with the immediate danger of martyrdom having been lifted, they were to now conduct their life as *living martyrs*, those who were alive unto God but dead to the things of the world. Many of the Christians who were formerly persecuted began to move to the deserts by the thousands.[60] Eventually, these Christians would seek out a spiritual leader, a spiritual mentor, similar to our modern-day version of a pastor. These Christians would form small communities centered around a wise, much older man who could offer wisdom, counsel, and inspiration in one's pursuit of God. The wise old man would be called *abbot* by those who considered themselves to be his disciples. *Abbot* is an Aramaic term that means "father." This movement gave rise to what became known as *monasticism*. Monasticism is a religious way of life in which one renounces worldly pursuits to devote oneself fully to spiritual work.

Monasticism in the fifth century in the Middle East produced some very interesting ministers with very unorthodox ministry styles that all centered around conducting their life as living martyrs. Despite their different methods of sharing the Gospel, these ministers were still very much anointed by the Holy Spirit in reaching the lost. One of these unusual types of ministries would be the *stylites*. No, this is not referring to hairstylists who take care of people's hair, but rather is a term used to describe those who are known as the *pillar saints*. The stylite was one who lived on top of a tall stone pillar and never came down, not even during the blistering desert heat of summer or the freezing cold of winter. The greatest of the stylites was Simeon the Elder. He spent forty-two years of his life mostly in a standing position on top of a pillar.

Simeon became a Christian at the age of thirteen after hearing the first sermon he ever heard preached, which was by a priest who taught on the words of Jesus, "Blessed are the pure in heart, for they will see God" (Matthew 5:8, NIV). This scripture became Simeon's life's theme, and it was incorporated into all of his sermons. He was allowed to join a monastery at the age of fifteen, but his austere practices were so hard that he was soon asked to leave. He became a hermit living on the side of a mountain, but because of his deep walk with God, people would come to him in ever-increasing numbers, seeking his prayers and counsel. Simeon often heard an angelic voice telling him to "dig even deeper." His quest for spiritual depth would soon take him on a new journey that led him on an upward path.

In order to find a means by which he could pray as often as possible, carry out his fleshly mortifications, and also minister to those who needed spiritual help, he built a pillar in an abandoned field near the village of Telanissa (located in modern-day Syria). He made the top of the pillar his new base of operation. The pillar that Simeon built was about nine feet in height and had a small platform on top that was about one square meter.

Because of his preaching style of delivering two practical messages daily, his ability to settle disputes through love and wise counsel, and his connection with God through which many prayer requests of the people being given to him were answered in miraculous ways, the crowds again began to come to him in his remote location. When the Desert Fathers (the bishops and abbots) living in the southern Negev heard about his new style of ministry, they wondered if Simeon was doing it out of a pure heart or perhaps to draw attention to himself. Was it a case of pride or humility? The younger monks in Egypt thought that Simeon was seeking attention. Some of the archimandrites (the religious heads of large monasteries) in Antioch denounced Simeon as an attention grabber. The Desert Fathers wanted to test Simeon, so they ordered him under obedience to come down from the pillar. Upon hearing the command, Simeon came down immediately, responding in absolute obedience to those whom he viewed as leaders in the Christian faith. His obedience touched the hearts of the Christian leaders, and they decided to allow Simeon to continue peacefully with his unusual method of ministry.

Over the years, the crowds grew larger around Simeon's little pillar. Arabs, Persians, Armenians, Spanish, and those from various parts of modern-day Britain and France journeyed as Christian pilgrims to hear him preach and ask for spiritual guidance. Princes and queens from throughout the Middle East came to receive his blessing. The Persian ruler King Bahram V greatly respected Simeon, although he was a pagan king. Roman Emperors Theodosius the Younger and Leo I the Thracian often consulted Simeon on difficult matters. Emperor Marcian went so far as to visit Simeon, disguised in the dress of a common man. It was Simeon who wisely counseled Empress Eudoxia to break away from the heretical group known as the Entychians, a group who denied that there was a difference between human and divine nature.

After four years on his nine-foot-tall pillar, Simeon moved to consecutively taller pillars that were built for him by the local people. His second pillar was twelve feet tall, and he lived there for three years. He then moved to his third pillar that was thirty-six feet tall, and he stayed there for ten years. Finally, he moved to his fourth pillar that was sixty feet tall, and he lived there for the last twenty-five years of his life. The top of his pillar had a flat platform that wasn't larger than three feet in diameter, making it impossible for him to stretch himself out upon. His pillar home had no roof, no walls, and only a short balustrade going around the side to keep him from being blown off during strong winds. He wore a leather garment, had long hair and a beard, and ate very little food or drink. He spent most of his nights standing up in prayer and worship. Often in his nightly prayers, he would stand praying and would bow frequently and low. One witness said he stopped counting after seeing Simeon bow 1,244 times in his nightly prayer.

After living and preaching on top of a pillar for forty-two years, Simeon's life ended at the age of sixty-nine. One of his young assistants named Antonius noticed that Simeon had not moved, so he went up on a tall later to check on him. The assistant said,

> When he did not answer me, I thought I would not say anything to anyone—I was frightened to touch him. After standing there for half an hour I bent down to put my ear where I could listen more

closely. There was no breath, only a smell as of many perfumes which rose from his body, and I knew that he had gone to rest in the Lord. Stunned, I wept bitterly, bent down and kissed his eyes and smoothed his beard and the hair on his head.[61]

Perched on top of his pillar, Simeon was like a flame burning on top of a candle. He ministered to countless people while he lived, and after his death, he had influenced hundreds of other young ministers who, between the fifth and seventh centuries, also became pillar preachers. As Simeon was living out his last few days on earth, the Syriac Vita records that a sweet and cooling breeze settled around his pillar: "several odors were different from one another, so that neither spices nor sweet herbs and pleasant smells which are in the world, can be compared to the fragrance."[62]

The principles of monasticism eventually developed into monasteries (a monastic community), with monks (unmarried men who desire to devote their lives completely to God), nuns (unmarried women who choose to stay single to devote their life in service to the Lord), and other expressions that involved a primary focus of spreading the gospel while remaining as detached as possible from the world. Monasteries were centers of religious learning that also taught the illiterate public how to read and write. As monasteries grew in size, they eventually had communities form around them, which developed into towns. The Old English word for "monastery" is *minister*. Towns in England today that end with the word *minster* or have that word attached to them indicate that they were once religious communities that grew up around monasteries. We see this in towns such as Westminster, Upminster, Minster Lovell, Southminster, and many others.

Many Christian theologians believe that monasticism reached its fullest expression through the Irish saints, who would undoubtedly be considered some of the toughest, hardiest saints to ever walk the face of the earth. They delighted in hardships, persecution, and hostile environments. They were well-skilled in the Scriptures, and they could also flow in the anointing of the Holy Spirit with countless miracles performed in the name of the Lord. Such rugged individuals as St. Patrick, St. Brendan, St. Columba, St. Brigid, St. Kevin, and St. Finnian not only influenced Ireland, but they were successful in spreading the gospel throughout Ireland, Scotland, continental Europe, and to other parts of the world.

The early Irish saints taught the concept that you are an island, and although there may be much going on around you, yet your closeness to God produces an inner communion and nearness to God, making your life be just as if you lived alone on a remote island. Indeed, some of them did choose rugged islands upon which to establish their monasteries. Saint Columba (his name means "Dove") was Irish, but he moved to the island of Iona off the west coast of Scotland with his twelve disciples in AD 563. There he raised up a monastery that became a great hub of educational learning and missionary outreach. Saint Aiden (his name means "Little Fiery One") was an Irishman, a monk, and a spiritual son of Saint Columba. King Oswald of Northumberland in North East England had requested that the monastery on Iona send him a missionary. Aiden was the man for the assignment, and he chose the tidal island of Lindisfarne for his ministry base. The island is cut off from the mainland at high tide, but it was the perfect place for the establishment of a monastery. Over time the monastery grew and had a major impact in spreading the Gospel to Britain; it is recognized today by scholars and historians as being the "cradle of Christianity" in England.

Saint Columba (December 521–June 597) converting King Brude of the Picts to Christianity. This mural painting by William Hole is in the Scottish National Portrait Gallery

The majority of the Irish monastic saints and Desert Fathers were ascetics. An ascetic is someone who practices extreme self-denial or self-mortification to crucify their flesh nature. An ascetic is a person who leads a very simple life, abstains from the normal pleasures of life, and denies himself or herself the basic comforts that most people enjoy. For example, Saint Columba slept on a stone slab and used a large rock for a pillow. Saint Kevin was also an ascetic. He lived in the sixth century and was born of Irish royalty. He chose at a young age to live as a hermit in a small cave, spending his life in prayer and self-denial to worldly interests. Similar to Columba, he also chose to sleep on a stone floor and used a rock as a pillow. He lived off herbs, walked barefoot, and prayed for many hours each day, with one hour of prayer and psalm reading being done while standing in a lake with the cold icy water up past his waist. Many of the Irish saints prayed through the entire 150 psalms in the Old Testament on a daily basis. Kelly and I have had the privilege of visiting the remnants of St. Kevin's ancient monastery in the lush green valley of Glendalough, Ireland. It is truly a beautiful place.

Fasting and prayer were a central part of devotion for all Irish saints. Saint Patrick is well known for having hiked barefoot to the top of the mountain, now known as Croagh Patrick. There he prayed and fasted for forty days. Today, every year, on the last weekend of July, over 30,000 pilgrims still make the hike to the top of the mountain. Recently Kelly and I happened to be in Ireland during that particular weekend, and we joined in with the crowd of pilgrims to make our way slowly to the summit. We noticed quite a few hearty souls who were trying to make the journey barefoot. Only a few succeeded who tried it in this manner: the sharp rocks and loose gravel make it almost impossible. Kelly and I talked to one Irish gentleman in his early eighties who had just completed another hike to the top and back with no shoes on. He said he has now done the hike barefoot forty-four times. His rugged appearance looked to me like he was made of a mixture of steel and leather, certainly a hardy Irishman if I have ever seen one.

Long fasts and a disciplined prayer life were a standard operating procedure for the Irish saints. Their spiritual hunger produced a deep walk with God and some remarkable writings that have influenced generations of truth seekers. One of these famous writings is the prayer known as The Deer's Cry. This prayer was composed by Saint Patrick in AD 433. Patrick was aware that an ambush had been set to try and kill him and his entire group. They were traveling to the Hill of Tara to meet King Loegaire and his court early in the morning. It was during the march that they sang the Deer's Cry. The druids (a pagan group of priests who practiced occultism and human sacrifice) were hiding in the bushes, ready to kill them. The miracle is that they never saw Patrick and his men, only a gentle doe passing by, followed by twenty fawns. God saved Patrick and his men by concealing them from the enemy. The Deer's Cry is also known as The Breastplate of St. Patrick. This prayer is often used as a prayer of protection.

I arise today through a mighty strength, the invocation of the Trinity, through belief in the Threeness, through confession of the Oneness of the Creator of creation.

I arise today through the strength of Christ with His Baptism,

through the strength of His Crucifixion with His Burial

through the strength of His Resurrection with His Ascension,

through the strength of His descent for the Judgment of Doom.

I arise today through the strength of the love of Cherubim

in obedience of Angels, in the service of the Archangels,

in hope of resurrection to meet with reward,

in prayers of Patriarchs, in predictions of Prophets,

in preaching's of Apostles, in faiths of Confessors,

in innocence of Holy Virgins, in deeds of righteous men.

I arise today, through the strength of Heaven:

light of Sun, brilliance of Moon, splendor of Fire,

speed of Lightning, swiftness of Wind, depth of Sea,

stability of Earth, firmness of Rock.

I arise today, through God's strength to pilot me:

God's might to uphold me, God's wisdom to guide me,

God's eye to look before me, God's ear to hear me,

God's word to speak for me, God's hand to guard me,

God's way to lie before me, God's shield to protect me,

God's host to secure me:

against snares of devils, against temptations of vices,

against inclinations of nature, against everyone who

shall wish me ill, afar and anear, alone and in a crowd.

I summon today all these powers between me (and these evils):

against every cruel and merciless power that may oppose

my body and my soul,

against incantations of false prophets,

against black laws of heathenry,

against false laws of heretics, against craft of idolatry,

against spells of witches and smiths and wizards,

against every knowledge that endangers man's body and soul.

Christ to protect me today

against poison, against burning, against drowning,

against wounding, so that there may come abundance of reward.

Christ with me, Christ before me, Christ behind me, Christ in me,

Christ beneath me, Christ above me, Christ on my right,

Christ on my left, Christ in breadth, Christ in length,

Christ in height, Christ in the heart of every man who thinks of me,

Christ in the mouth of every man who speaks of me,

Christ in every eye that sees me, Christ in every ear that hears me.

I arise today through a mighty strength, the invocation of the

Trinity, through belief in the Threeness, through confession of the

Oneness of the Creator of creation.

Salvation is of the Lord. Salvation is of the Lord.

Salvation is of Christ. May Thy Salvation, O Lord, be ever with us.[63]

Patrick on his way to Tara, attended by those he converted to Christ, including his youthful convert Benignus who became one of his most beloved disciples

In a true story that runs very similarly to the clash of Elijah the prophet with the false prophets of Baal on Mount Carmel, Patrick appeared before the Irish king to share the gospel with him on the Hill of Tara during a festival known as "Baal's fire." The ancient Irish were a fierce people, with a well-earned reputation for being wild, dark, terrible, and savage in their behavior. Patrick risked his life by interrupting this annual night of Satan worship in order to bring the gospel of Christ to those who had never heard it. Gathered were the king and his royal court, the Druid priests with their black flags, the chieftains of the land and their clans, the influential bards, and countless multitudes of common people from every province of Ireland. This epic moment is recounted to us by the Celtic historian and gifted writer Dr. James A. Wiley, who drew upon old manuscripts to provide us with an insight into what happened on that night.

The monarch beheld in Patrick a man plain in dress, like one who dwelt more in the wilderness than in cities, his features roughened by exposure to sun and storm, yet stamped with an air of great dignity. On his brow the close-knit gathered lines of resolve; in his eye the fire of a lofty zeal; his voice strung with energy; his words courageous, but calm and wise; every step and movement of his person betokening self-possession. No such man had Logaire ever before looked upon. Rugged, weather-beaten though he was, no one of all the Druids at his court had ever inspired him with such awe as this prophet-like man. He must hear what he has to say. The king motions to the courtiers to stand aside and let the strange figure approach; he bids the Druids be still. There is silence, and Patrick speaks. Respectfully, yet not flatteringly, fearlessly, yet not offensively, does Patrick address Logaire. To know what is in man is to possess the secret of moving and ruling him. Patrick knew that in the heart of the monarch, as in that of the serf, is a deep-seated sense of guiltiness, and an equally deep-seated foreboding of punishment, and that no sooner does reason unfold than this burden begins to press. It is a shadow that will not depart. [...]

He asks them whether it is not these fears this pale specter which has driven them to the altars and sacrifices of the Druid? Whether they have not sought these bloody oblations in the vague hope of expiation and relief? Well, have you found the rest you seek? At the altar of the Druid, has the sense of guilt left you? Has the blood that streams on it washed out the stain? If you shall permit your hearts to speak, they will answer, No, the sin is still unpurged, and the terror is still unconquered. Why multiply rites which are as profitless as they are cruel? Flee from these altars whereon never yet came victim that could avail for expiation. Cease from these sacrifices of blood, which pollute, but do not cleanse, the offeror.

Listen to me. I will tell you of a better altar, and a greater Priest, a Priest who has opened to you the road to the skies. I will tell you of a Father who sent His Son to be a sacrifice in your place. That Son, having offered His sacrifice, and returned from the tomb, as the conqueror of death, has ascended into the heavens, and now sits on the right hand of His Father, the crown of an everlasting dominion on His head. He is sending His ambassadors to all nations to proclaim that there is not a wanderer on the face of the earth, there is not one of the sons of men, the humblest, the vilest, the guiltiest, who is not welcome to return, and who shall not be received by the Father, coming by that Priest, who, having no sin of His own, was able to make a real and complete expiation of the sin of others.[64]

Patrick continued to share the gospel with the large assembly of people. Although the king remained unconverted, the queen and the two royal daughters put their trust in Christ. The next day the king's brother, Connal, confessed that he had also become a Christian. Dubbach, the chief of the bards and one of the greatest poets in Ireland, also converted. Despite the king's willingness to hold to his old religion, his passion for it was no longer there. Seeing that Patrick's message was not a threat to his own throne, he allowed Patrick to preach unhindered throughout his dominion. Ireland's shift from paganism to Christianity had begun, and the nation would never be the same again.

Many of the Irish people embraced the Christian faith and left their dark superstitious past, and became holy and prosperous people in Christ. While much of Africa and the Middle East would soon slip into the emerging grip of Islam, and while Europe was still in bondage to ancient forms of idolatry and ongoing revolutions, yet history records how Ireland rose to be a shining light of evangelism by sending forth missionaries to distant lands, erecting schools and colleges, teaching the Scriptures, and building churches. The Welsh monk and historian Nennius writing in the ninth century said that Patrick accomplished in his lifetime the founding of three hundred and sixty-five churches, the ordination of three hundred and sixty-five bishops, and the training of three thousand elders. Anytime Patrick planted a church, he also planted a school. In this way, the knowledge of God increased, and civilization moved forward at an equal pace. Through the acceptance of the gospel brought by Patrick, Ireland became the foremost lamp of light to the nations of the world for the next seven hundred years.

Ancient Irish texts speak of three forms of martyrdom: white, green, and red. White martyrdom meant separation from the world and the embracing of a life that centered on prayer and fasting. Green martyrdom meant you engaged in all aspects of white martyrdom, plus you were an ascetic who practiced extreme forms of self-mortification for the purpose of crucifying the flesh nature and developing a keen awareness of the presence of God. Red martyrdom meant you practiced all elements of white and green martyrdom, and you suffered persecution and eventually death for your faith in Christ. When you study the martyrs of the early church, you find written testimony of the "odor of sanctity" that would appear during the life and deaths of many devout Christians. When you research the lives of the early monastic saints, the same manifestation of supernatural fragrance can be found in numerous testimonies. For example, at the death of Saint Patrick, it was written, "An odor of ravishing sweetness filled the room where the body was laid out."[65]

For the fragrance of Christ to emanate from you, it requires (a) exposure to the deeper things of God. You will have to push past the superficial and mundane form of living that so many Christians have chosen to accept. Glimpses into the lives of various saints, which are a form of exposure, demonstrate that if they can experience an exceptional touch of His grace, then you too can know a richer and more fulfilling relationship with the Lord. Manifesting the fragrance of Christ also requires that (b) you must be willing to live a life that is fully surrendered to the Lord by observing all the commandments of God, thus demonstrating the reality of being a living martyr. This comes down to connecting with the same principles that guided the apostles and prophets of the early church, who could all agree with the words of Apostle Paul: "I affirm, by the boasting in you which I have in Christ Jesus our Lord, I die daily" (1 Corinthians 15:31).

The putting to death of the flesh nature is a daily requirement for those who want to walk in the fragrance of Christ. The devil can offer many areas of temptation to a Christian, but in order to do so, he has to contact the believer through some form of their five physical senses.

When the physical senses of the flesh are crucified, then the devil has no door of access into the life of a Christian. This dying to self can be worked out in different ways. It may be as simple but deeply profound as never eating all you want. While this may sound easy to do, we all know that it is extremely difficult to fulfill, especially when food is plentiful and the flavors are exceptional. But just following this one discipline can propel a believer forward into a greater awareness of the Lord's presence and the leading of the Holy Spirit.

When you combine the two qualities of (a) ongoing exposure to the deeper and more fulfilling things of God with a life of (b) obedience to God's commandments that demonstrates you are alive to God and dead to the sinful world, you are then positioned to step into not only supernatural fragrances but into every other blessing of God as well. Upon your acceptance of these conditions, it is then time for you to release your faith and believe that supernatural fragrances will begin to be activated in your life. Apostle Paul told the church in Rome: "For I long to see you, that I may impart to you some spiritual gift, so that you may be established" (Romans 1:11).

Paul revealed that spiritual gifts can be imparted by those who are walking in them. We see the same principle applied when Jesus spoke to His twelve apostles and said: "Freely you have received, freely give" (Matthew 10:8).

I would like to ask you to find a quiet place where you can kneel before the Lord in prayer to receive this gift. Please verbally pray it out loud as we agree together in faith for God to grant you this request. Here is my prayer for you:

"Dear heavenly Father, I pray for my brother or sister in the Lord who is reading this. I ask that You impart to them the grace to operate in the gift of experiencing supernatural fragrances by the power of the Holy Spirit. I ask in the name of Jesus that You open their prophetic senses to allow them to smell in the spirit. Let the spiritual gift of discerning of spirits come forth now in their life, for Your glory. Let a new anointing come upon them now, and by Your grace may this new anointing be sustained by a close walk with You.

I thank You, Father, for a breakthrough for them into this prophetic realm. I thank You that their joy will be full and that their witness will be powerful, turning many that are lost to Christ while encouraging the faithful. Father, we thank You for this, and we give You praise. We call it done, in Jesus's name. Amen."

As an act of faith, lift up your hands and praise the Lord and shout, "I have received it; it is mine, in Jesus's name." Be mindful that this gift can manifest at any time for the Christian, sometimes when you least expect it. If nothing happens immediately, it doesn't mean you didn't receive it. Just enjoy life and walk closely with the Lord, and you will have times when this gift will manifest, and you will smell supernatural fragrances. This gift can also be developed with greater frequency and intensity through a strong devotional life of prayer, fasting, and a life that honors the Lord through obedience to His commandments. May you have many encounters with the Lord in the area of supernatural fragrance!

Prayer to Receive Salvation in Jesus Christ, Instructions for Water Baptism, and Prayer for the Infilling of the Holy Spirit

Perhaps you came across this book and have not yet had the opportunity to personally receive Jesus Christ as Savior and Lord. I would like to invite you to open your heart to Him now. Please read the following verses from the Bible out loud. When you vocalize Bible verses, it allows bold faith to enter your heart.

Seek the LORD while He may be found,

Call upon Him while He is near.

Let the wicked forsake his way,

And the unrighteous man his thoughts;

Let him return to the LORD,

And He will have mercy on him;

And to our God,

For He will abundantly pardon.

Isaiah 55:6-7

All of us have become like one who is unclean,

and all our righteous acts are like filthy rags;

we all shrivel up like a leaf,

and like the wind our sins sweep us away.

Isaiah 64:6 (NIV)

"For God loved the world so much that he gave his one and only Son, so that everyone who believes in him will not perish but have eternal life" (John 3:16, NLT).

"And it shall come to pass that whoever calls on the name of the LORD shall be saved" (Acts 2:21).

"There is salvation in no one else! God has given no other name under heaven by which we must be saved" (Acts 4:12, NLT).

"For all have sinned, and come short of the glory of God" (Romans 8:23).

"If you confess with your mouth that Jesus is Lord and believe in your heart that God raised him from the dead, you will be saved" (Romans 10:9, NLT).

Now that you have read how you may be saved, you can obey the Word of God and make your life right with God. Simply pray the following prayer from your heart with sincerity, and Jesus will give you His eternal life.

"Dear Lord Jesus, today I choose to make You my Lord and Savior. I confess that You are the Son of God. I believe that You were raised from the dead and are alive forevermore. Because of my sin, I have been separated from God, but You died on the cross and rose to life again to make it possible for me to be forgiven. While on the cross, You paid the price for my sin. You have made it possible for me to now receive forgiveness of sins. Today, I choose to receive Your forgiveness and grace. Come into my heart and forgive me of all my sins. From this moment on, I surrender my life to follow You. I confess with my mouth that You are the Lord, the Son of God, and I receive You as my Lord and Savior."

Now lift your hands and begin to praise God. From the bottom of your heart, give Him thanks for saving you. Now that you belong to Jesus, your next step is to get baptized in water as soon as possible in obedience to the commandments of Jesus. You do not need to be baptized in order to be saved. We are saved by God's grace and through placing our faith in Him. However, water baptism is an "outward sign" of this "inward work" of grace. It symbolizes our trust in the death, burial, and resurrection of Jesus.

Water Baptism Instructions

"And now why are you waiting? Arise and be baptized, and wash away your sins, calling on the name of the Lord" (Acts 22:16).

After having received Christ into your heart, you should be water baptized in order to publicly profess your faith in Jesus Christ.

Baptism is the next step that identifies you as a disciple of Jesus Christ. It provides an opportunity for you to make a simple profession of your faith before the church. You can invite friends and family to witness your confession of faith in Jesus.

According to Scripture, you should be water baptized in order to symbolize your cleansing from sin. Throughout the New Testament, baptism indicates that a person has "repented" or "turned away" from sin and works of darkness. Apostle Peter writes that the waters of baptism symbolize the cleansing of our conscience, not the cleansing of our body from dirt.

The term "baptize" literally means "to immerse or plunge." Going completely underwater best represents what happens when you become a Christian. As you go down into the water, you identify with spiritual death, and as you come up out of the water, you identify with the new spiritual life that you now have in Christ.

Ask a mature Christian who is faithfully following Jesus to baptize you. Perhaps it's a family member or close friend who has mentored you in this process of coming to Christ. Find an area of water deep enough to be submerged in: it could be a pool, river, lake, at the beach, or wherever there is ample water. The baptizer can be with you in the water. If it helps, you can plug your nose with one hand and grab your wrist with your other hand so that you don't swallow any water. The baptizer will say: "Do you believe that Jesus is the Christ, the Son of the living God, and do you claim Him as your personal Lord and Savior?"

You will then respond: "I do."

The baptizer will then say: "Upon your confession of faith, I now baptize you in the name of the Father and of the Son and the Holy Spirit."

He or she will then dunk you completely under the water. Once you are baptized, take time to celebrate by praising and worshipping the Lord. You may want to mark this moment in your Bible or journal as a way to record this milestone in your journey with Christ.

Instructions and Prayer to Receive the Infilling of the Holy Spirit

After salvation and after you have been water baptized, you need to allow Jesus to fill you to overflowing with His Holy Spirit. The following scriptures speak of being filled with the Holy Spirit and speaking in other tongues.

"And they were all filled with the Holy Spirit and began to speak with other tongues, as the Spirit gave them utterance" (Acts 2:4).

"When Paul had laid his hands upon them, the Holy Spirit came on them; and they spoke with tongues, and prophesied" (Acts 19:6).

Now ask the heavenly Father to fill you with His Holy Spirit by praying the following prayer: "Heavenly Father, please fill me with Your precious Holy Spirit so that I may speak in tongues and worship You all the days of my life. Let me receive the fullness of Your Spirit now."

Open your mouth and begin to speak in the new heavenly language that the Holy Spirit has given you. Let a new utterance come forth, not your own language, but the language the Holy Spirit gives you. Don't be concerned about how it sounds. It might not make sense to your mind, but it is your spirit communicating with God, and God understands everything you are speaking. Speak this out for one minute without stopping. Whenever you speak in tongues, you will find that God will strengthen and refresh you.

Praise the Lord! You are now a Spirit-filled Christian. Every day, speak in tongues so that you will be strong in your walk with God. Ask your heavenly Father to help you find a new church home so that you can grow spiritually and continue your spiritual pilgrimage toward heaven. The Holy Spirit will lead you as you search for the Christian church that God wants you to be a part of. Look for a church where you can sense the love of God and where people take a genuine interest in your spiritual growth. Seek out a church that believes the whole Bible and preaches it without compromise. And always remember *that God loves you.*

Notes

1 Daven Hiskey, "Did People in Medieval Times Really not Bathe?" Today I Found Out, August 26, 2019, http://www.todayifoundout. com/index.php/2019/08/did-people-in-medieval-times-really-not-bathe/.

2 "Napoleon, Josephine and a Giant Bill for Cologne…" Perfume Society, accessed May 17, 2021, https://perfumesociety.org/history/napoleon-josephine-and-a-giant-bill-for-cologne/.

3 Jeeves, "Ernest Beaux, Chanel and the Chanel N°5/Chanel N°5— for the first time—Inside Chanel," "Tweedland" The Gentlemen's club (blog), October 13, 2016, http://tweedlandthegentlemansclub.blogspot.com/2016/10/ernest-beaux-chanel-and-chanel-n5. html.

4 Hock Eng Khoo, Azrina Azlan, Sou Teng Tang, and See Meng Lim, "Anthocyanidins and anthocyanins: colored pigments as food, pharmaceutical ingredients, and the potential health benefits," August 13, 2017, https://www.ncbi.nlm.nih.gov/pmc/articles/ PMC5613902/.

5 Catholic News Agency, "Our Lady of Laus," May 6, 2008, YouTube video, https://youtu.be/Ka4prfsb-n4.

6 "Thieves' Oil: History—Recipes—Uses," Survival School, accessed May 17, 2021, https://survivalschool.com/%EF%BB%B-Fthieves-oil-history-recipes-uses/.

7 Charles Haddon Spurgeon, *The Complete Works* of C. H. Spurgeon, Volume 9, "No. 541: Direction in Dilemma," (Delmarva Publications, Inc., 2012), https://books.google.com/books?id=D-DZcCgAAQBAJ.

8 Morris Jastrow, Jr., Ira Maurice Price, Marcus Jastrow, Louis Ginzberg, "Brazen Sea," Jewish Encyclopedia, accessed May 17, 2021, http://www.jewishencyclopedia.com/articles/3659-brazen-sea.

9 Ebenezer Cobham Brewer, *A Dictionary of Miracles* (London:

Chatto and Windus, 1901), 510.

10 Ebenezer, 511

11 Ebenezer, 511.

12 Ebenezer, 511–512.

13 Ebenezer, 512.

14 St. Thérèse of Lisieux, *Story of a Soul*, Project Gutenberg, last updated January 3, 2009, https://www.gutenberg.org/cache/epub/16772/pg16772.html.

15 "Religion: Miracle Woman," *Time*, accessed May 17, 2021, http://content.time.com/time/subscriber/article/0,33009,902774,00.html.

16 "Kathryn Kuhlman," Christian Life Ministries, accessed May 17, 2021, https://www.christianlifeministries.com.au/people-of-faith/kathryn-kuhlman/.

17 Tony Francis, "Kathryn Kuhlman Miraculous Last Hours at the Hospital," June 22, 2020, YouTube video, https://youtu.be/-W22Cu_c1c8.

18 Menachem Posner, "Is It Special to Pass Away on One's Birthday?" Chabad-Lubavitch Media Center, accessed May 17, 2021, https://www.chabad.org/library/article_cdo/aid/1452114/jewish/Is-It-Special-to-Pass-Away-on-Ones-Birthday.htm.

19 Pamela Rosewell, *The Five Silent Years of Corrie ten Boom* (Grand Rapids, Mich: 1986), 170–171.

20 "Padre Pio's celestial perfumes," Padre Pio Foundation, accessed May 17, 2021, paragraph 3, http://www.padrepiofoundation.com/perfumes.htm.

21 Francesco Castelli, *Padre Pio Under Investigation, The Secret Vatican Files* (San Francisco: Ignatius Press, 2011), 124–125.

22 Charles Mortimer, Carty, Padre Pio: *The Stigmatist* (Charlotte, North Carolina: TAN Books, 1994), 35.

23 "Padre Pio's celestial perfumes," paragraph 10.

24 "Padre Pio's celestial perfumes," paragraph 15.

25 "Padre Pio's celestial perfumes," paragraph 16.

26 "Padre Pio's celestial perfumes," paragraph 14.

27 Joan Carroll Cruz, *Mysteries, Marvels and Miracles: In the Lives of the Saints* (Charlotte, North Carolina: TAN Books, 1997), 67.

28 *The Life of the Blessed Paul of the Cross, Founder of the Congregation of the Barefooted Clerks, and Of the Most Holy Cross and Passion of Jesus Christ* (1856), volume 3, 5–6.

29 Cruz, 82.

30 Paolo Agelli, *Joseph of Copertino* (CreateSpace Independent Publishing Platform, 2014), 188–190.

31 Agelli, 188–190.

32 Agelli, 188–190.

33 Agelli, 188–190.

34 Agelli, 188–190.

35 Agelli, 188–190.

36 Agelli, 188–190.

37 "Blessed Mother Teresa on Abortion," Catholic News Agency, accessed May 17, 2021, https://www.catholicnewsagency.com/resource/55399/blessed-mother-teresa-on-abortion.

38 *Ecclesiastical History*, quoted by John Piper, "By What Death Will You Glorify God?" DesiringGod, September 1, 1999, https://www.desiringgod.org/articles/by-what-death-will-you-glorify-god.

39 Ibn Ezra, *Commentary of Ibn Ezra on Isaiah* (ca. 1155–ca. 1165 CE), Sefaria, accessed May 17, 2021, https://www.sefaria.org/Ibn_Ezra_on_Isaiah.11.3?lang=bi.

40 Ephraim Nissan, Abraham Ofir Shemesh, "Olfaction When Judging, According To Isaiah 11:3-4," *Bibbia e Oriente* (2017, issue

4), 3.

41 John Calvin, *John Calvin's Commentary on the Bible* (Calvin Translation Society, 1850), https://books.google.com/books?id=Nyw5AQAAMAAJ.

42 Dictionary.com, LLC, s.v. "Discernment," accessed May 17, 2021, https://www.dictionary.com/browse/discernment.

43 Thomas Arnold, *The Select Works of John Wyclif* (Oxford: The Clarendon Press, 1869), volume 1, 107–108.

44 Maimonides (Rambam), *Guide for the Perplexed* (1190 CE), Sefaria, accessed May 17, 2021, https://www.sefaria.org/Guide_for_the_Perplexed?lang=bi.

45 Siddur Ashkenaz, (ca. 1055–ca. 1105 CE), Sefaria, accessed June 24, 2021, https://www.sefaria.org/Siddur_Ashkenaz%2C_Weekday%2C_Shacharit%2C_Preparatory_Prayers%2C_Korbanot%2C_Ketoret.4?ven=Translation_based_on_the_Metsudah_linear_siddur,_by_Avrohom_Davis,_1981&lang=bi.

46 Tractate Kereisos, Schottenstein Edition, quoted in "Preparation of the Incense and View of the Avtinas Chamber," Beis Hamikdash (blog), February 17, 2014, https://www.beishamikdashtopics.com/2014/02/preparation-of-incense-and-view-of.html.

47 Alfred Edersheim, *Temple, Its Ministry and Service* (Religious Tract Society, 2006), 138.

48 Shmuel Tzvi-Hirsch Glick, *Ein Yaakov* (Chicago, 1921), Sefaria, accessed May 17, 2021, https://www.sefaria.org/Ein_Yaakov_(Glick_Edition)?lang=bi.

49 Rivkah Lambert Adler, "Stash of Original Temple Incense Found," Israel365 News, March 18, 2019, https://www.israel-365news.com/124843/stash-original-temple-incense-found/.

50 Dr. T. Hutter, "Palynological Assessment of 'the Qumran Spices,'" May 15, 1994, 53.

51 Talmud Yoma, the William Davidson Talmud (ca. 450–ca. 550

CE), Sefaria, accessed June 24, 2021, https://www.sefaria.org/Yoma?lang=bi&p2=Yoma.38a.14&lang2=en.

52 Wikipedia, s.v. "Diocletianic Persecution," last modified May 7, 2021, https://en.wikipedia.org/wiki/Diocletianic_Persecution.

53 Eusebius. *History of the Church*, quoted in "The Letter of the Churchs of Vienna and Lyons to the Churches of Asia and Phrygia including the story of the Blessed Blandina," Internet History Sourcebooks, the History Department of Fordham University, accessed May 17, 2021, https://sourcebooks.fordham.edu/source/177-lyonsmartyrs.asp.

54 Eusebius. *History of the Church*, quoted in "A Letter From the Suffering Church in Gaul—c. 175 AD," Silouan Thompson, August 4, 2008, https://silouanthompson.net/2008/08/letterfromgaul/.

55 Eusebius. *History of the Church*, quoted in "The Letter of the Churchs of Vienna and Lyons."

56 Eusebius. *History of the Church*, quoted in "A Letter From the Suffering Church in Gaul—c. 175 AD."

57 Eusebius. *History of the Church*, quoted in "The Letter of the Churchs of Vienna and Lyons."

58 Eusebius. *History of the Church*, quoted in "A Letter From the Suffering Church in Gaul—c. 175 AD."

59 Eusebius. *History of the Church*, quoted in "The Letter of the Churchs of Vienna and Lyons."

60 Marina Miladinov, *Margins of Solitude: Eremitism in Central Europe between East and West* (Zagreb: Leykam International, 2008).

61 Antony, *Vitae Patrum Life No 10: The Life of St Simeon Stylites by Antony, his disciple* quoted by Coptic Place, accessed May 17, 2021, http://www.copticplace.com/Saints_E/Lives_of_Saints/Simeon.html.

62 Frederick Lent, *The Life of St. Simeon Stylites*, JSTOR, https://www.jstor.org/stable/592644, 189.

63 "A Saint Patrick's Day Prayer," Redemption Church, March 17, 2020, https://www.redemption.cc/blog/a-saint-patricks-day-prayer.

64 James Aitken Wylie, *History of the Scottish Nation* (Library of Alexandria, 1890), https://books.google.com/books?id=PCjFD-D9gQGYC.

65 Ebenezer, 511.

About Pastor Steven Brooks

Pastor Steven is a husband, father, minister, and best-selling author who is a prophetic revealer of spiritual realities within the kingdom of God. He is widely known for his ability to teach God's Word with depth and in a clear and understandable way to new believers as well as to those who have been in the faith for decades. The Holy Spirit moves in wonderful ways as he ministers, causing the oil of joy to flow abundantly and for all manner of burdens, yokes, and spiritual chains to be destroyed. He operates strongly in all nine gifts of the Spirit, with a remarkable anointing in the area of discerning of spirits and the working of miracles. Supernatural signs and wonders follow him as he ministers, and many people are drawn into a hunger for a deeper walk with God.

Along with his wife Kelly, he has traveled throughout the world ministering the Word of God while also daily reaching out to multitudes of souls through their half-hour television program called *Pure Gold*. Pastor Steven's messages are watched in many nations on various internet platforms, as well as through many branches of social media. His books continue to make an impact around the world, having been translated from English into Russian, Mandarin Chinese, Korean, Spanish, Indonesian, and other languages.

Pure Gold Covenant Partners

If you have been blessed by this book, we would like to invite you to become a Pure Gold covenant partner with Steven Brooks International. Although you may already have a home church to which you belong, you may also wish to partner with and financially support Pastor Steven's ministry with a regular donation each month. If this is your desire, then please consider the mutual blessing of partnering with us in the Lord's kingdom work as a Pure Gold covenant partner.

Partnership is a divine connection where the anointing on this ministry is transferred upon your life by the Spirit of God. In professional powerlifting, where strong men lift heavy weights, it is understood that it takes more than large muscles to move such poundage. It also requires other equally important components such as well-developed ligaments and tendons, mental focus, and perfect balance. Everything in the whole body has to work together to lift the weight overhead in order to win the prize. It is the same way in the body of Christ. We all pull and lift together, and because of this, we also share equally in the rewards together.

It is through the prayers and gracious financial support of our Pure Gold covenant partners that Pastor Steven is able to reach into the nations of the world with a message that lifts people into the fullness of their destiny. His primary teaching thrust is to emphasize the importance of developing a close walk with God and how to exercise specific faith in God that produces constant and consistent victory.

When writing to the church in Philippi, the apostle Paul said, "You are all partakers of my grace" (Philippians 1:7). He was basically telling them that the blessing, anointing, revelation, and gifting that he walked in would operate in their lives also. A covenant relationship with God and an anointed minister of God is a key component to prospering and succeeding in life, as we see in the following verse: "Believe in the LORD your God, and you shall be established; believe His prophets, and you shall prosper" (2 Chronicles 20:20).

We call our loyal supporters Pure Gold covenant partners because they are the ones who help us carry the glory of God to the nations through our various ministry outreaches. Through books, conferences, the internet, social media, and our half-hour *Pure Gold* television program, we are sending the gospel to all the world. By definition, a covenant is a mutual agreement of two or more persons who come together to share their strengths in order to offset any weaknesses. For example, in biblical times, a fishing village might make a covenant with a nearby village of warriors. The fishing village needs protection, and the warriors need food, so there is a viable reason for joining forces. Covenant relationships are central to carrying out the Lord's plan for our lives.

Without the help of dedicated ministry partners, the great outreaches of this ministry would not be possible. The help of each ministry partner is vital because our strength is multiplied when we stand together as one. We cannot do what God has called us to do without your help, so let's synchronize our unique abilities and dare to do extraordinary exploits for the Lord.

Pastor Steven and Pastor Kelly absolutely treasure their Pure Gold covenant partners. Each one is viewed as a special gift from God who is to be highly valued. God is joining those with like hearts to stand together in this sacred work. Thank you for your desire to become a Pure Gold covenant partner. We encourage you to take the next step and join this exciting and rewarding journey with us. Together we are making an eternal difference in the lives of precious souls, enabling us to have an expectancy to hear the Lord's voice on that blessed day, saying, "Well done, good and faithful servant."

As a Pure Gold covenant partner, your undertaking is to pray for Pastor Steven, his family, and his ministry on a regular basis and support his ministry with a monthly financial contribution.

In return, you will receive the following benefits:

- Direct impartation that is upon Pastor Steven's life to be transferred upon you by the Holy Spirit, thus empowering you to fulfill the blessed assignment for which you were brought into the earth.

- Consistent prayer for you by Pastor Steven.
- Mutual faith in God for His best return on all your giving.
- An eternal and equal share in the heavenly rewards obtained through this ministry.

"The share of the one who goes into battle is to be the same as the share of the one who remains with the supplies. They will share equally" (words of King David expressing the spiritual law of covenant partnership; 1 Samuel 30:24).

To become a Pure Gold covenant partner, please fill out the form and submit it online, or mail it to us today along with your offering so that you can be enrolled as a Pure Gold covenant partner. You can also enroll online at www.stevenbrooks.org/partner.

First Name _____

Last Name _____

Mailing Address _____

City _____

State _____

Zip _____

Country _____

Email Address _____

Please Mail to:

Steven Brooks International

PO Box 717

Moravian Falls, NC. 28654

You may also become a Pure Gold covenant partner by registering at our online website at www.stevenbrooks.org.

Once there, please click on the "Partner" link to sign up.

For booking information and upcoming meetings regarding Steven Brooks International, please visit our website at www.stevenbrooks.org or email us at info@stevenbrooks.org.

Online Church with Pastor Steven Brooks!

Twice a week, Pastor Steven greets all online church members, ministry partners, and friends from around the world with his timely messages. Each sermon is carefully prepared through study and prayer, and the Holy Spirit pinpoints and provides the heavenly manna that is needed for each viewer. The answer to all human needs can be supplied through the Bible, which is the Word of God. As Pastor Steven ministers the Word, the knowledge of that word brings understanding, and a well-lit path is placed before the believer upon which to walk. Join us as we study God's Word, and through the application of that Word, you will begin to experience success and victory in all areas of your life.

The age of technological advancement gained through the internet has given a deeper meaning to the words of Jesus when He said, "For wherever two or three people come together in my name, I am there, right among you" (Matthew 18:20, Phillips).

Through the internet, we can assemble together and enjoy the presence of the Lord and His anointing as it flows from the studio, through the camera, and into your very home, car, or wherever you may be watching. Because this online church functions as a rich spiritual storehouse of knowledge and teaching, members also send in their tithes and offerings to honor the Lord with their finances, as the Scripture says:

> "Bring the full tenth into the storehouse so that there may be food in My house. Test Me in this way," says the LORD of Hosts. "See if I will not open the floodgates of heaven and pour out a blessing for you without measure."
>
> Malachi 3:10 (HCSB)

"And all the tithe (tenth part) of the land, whether the seed of the land or the fruit of the tree, is the Lord's; it is holy to the Lord" (Leviticus 27:30, AMP).

Tithing is the systematic giving of ten percent of all your increase to God. Tithing presents to you the wonderful opportunity to establish and fulfill your God-designed destiny. The benefits of tithing include prosperity, health, protection, and conformity into the mature image of Christ as promised by God when we meet His covenant conditions of honoring the Lord with our finances.

The great evangelist and founder of Methodism from the eighteenth century, John Wesley, claimed the world as his parish. He rode on horseback throughout England, covering over 250,000 miles, and often preached in public squares outside of traditional church settings. We also are inspired by the Holy Spirit to implement the same creative and expansive approach concerning ministry. Last year over a hundred countries visited our social media video channels to watch Pastor Steven's messages. Online church members are located all over North America, throughout Europe, Asia, Australia, and New Zealand, in communist countries, and in other nations where the church is fiercely persecuted. Pastor Steven's messages resonate with spiritually hungry believers around the world.

Some of the tremendous advantages of the Steven Brooks International online church are that it allows us to have a platform to reach an audience of unlimited size while also providing unique ministry opportunities for people to have church in countries where it is either illegal or life-threatening to attend a physical meeting. All messages are archived and are available for on-demand viewing. For the online member, the benefits are life-transforming as the presence and glory of God transcends distance and even time, entering your room regardless of where you live, ministering to you right where you are at.

We invite you to be a member of the Steven Brooks International online church. Become strong in faith, learn to flow in God's miracle power, walk in the blessings of God, and be filled to overflowing with the Spirit's life and joy!

Please click the link below to join if you are viewing this in an eBook format.

https://stevenbrooks.org/online-church/

Please submit your full contact information and mail it in to join:

Online Church Enrollment

First Name (required)

Last Name (required)

Address 1 (required)

Address 2

City (required)

Zip/Postal Code (required)

Email (required)

Please mail your information to:

Steven Brooks International

PO Box 717

Moravian Falls, NC. 28654

Testimonies from Online Church Members

"It's absolutely phenomenal how your messages speak to my heart and help me navigate through life!"

S. L.

"Just want to thank you for your amazing ministry! Each message is like a treasure chest filled with precious jewels, and I enjoy unpacking them. When listening to your messages, I have to wonder, 'Did the Lord let you into my house, like 2 Kings 6:12? Elisha in the bed-chamber? Or did you talk to my angel? Or discuss with my Lord about my situation?' Whatever it is, keep it up because your weekly messages are bringing greater understanding to me!"

S. S.

"I just had to let you know that I am so enjoying the messages that you preach! You have been such a tremendous blessing to me. I just found you a little over a month ago. Norvel Hayes was one of my favorite ministers. I was so deeply touched when he passed as I have been following him for years. When I found you, I felt God was adding you to my life as well. The way that you take time to explain the offering, prosperity before your messages, and then praying, building us up as well as teaching us, is just like nothing I have ever experienced. Then the Word is always a fresh word! It's as though you are reading my mail or looking into my heart and spirit and know what I need (the Holy Spirit is working through you for certain). I can see the gifts all being manifested through you. It is such a blessing. I listen to at least one or more of your sermons on a daily basis. You have inspired me to read more, study, and pray without ceasing. I am breaking through into a new realm on so many levels. Thank you for being transparent and explaining things on such an elementary level that even a schoolchild can understand. It is what God's people need.

"Also, I want to add...You are so funny in some of these sermons! You not only bless me with wisdom and knowledge, but you are just funny as well, explaining some things. That is a good thing. Laughter is like medicine. But it's a natural thing for you..."

T. W.

"Pastor Steven, I love to listen to your sermons and podcasts. I especially love to hear you speak of how to live daily with the Lord, as you do all the time. Few pastors go into such beautiful detail with personal references. It has been very helpful to me. Thank you for your willingness to do the Lord's work and to speak boldly for Him."

L. B.

"Pastor Steven, each year, I now do a Daniel's fast in January. The number of prayers answered and miracles that God has performed in the year have been astounding! I believe many of your teachings on fasting have helped play a role in that! We will be forever grateful to God for your amazing ministry!"

M. B.

"I feel like I know you so well, but you wouldn't know me from Adam! Do you know the very first time I heard my angel? It happened after I had been watching your archived show on Mantels, just before bed. Since then, Pastor Steven, I have watched almost every night, going back five years and watching all archived shows plus keeping up to date with the current ☺ My favorite show is how you and Kelly met!"

D. W.

"Hello Pastor Steven, in connection and response with your message on faith, called, 'The Violent Take It by Force,' I did a time of prayer and fasting. When my fast was ended, I was so hungry and thirsty that when I broke my fast, I asked the Lord for a coke soda. Would you believe after I said that, the young daughter of my Muslim neighbor knocked at my door? When I opened the door, she was holding a family-size bottle of coke. :-) And when I drank it, oh, the Lord just made me laugh :-) It was so out of this world. It was supernaturally tasty. Come to think of it, God used my Muslim neighbor for a bottle of family-size soda. :-)

"I followed your advice about seeking the Lord. I started doing my devotion on a daily basis of worshiping God, praying in tongues, and seriously studying the Word of God. I now get up at 4:30 am. I am seeing tremendous blessings coming my way. My husband got a pay raise. My boss emailed everyone in the building and commended me for doing an excellent job. My boss also said I am good at management. She doesn't know it :-) My secret weapon is getting up early while it is still dark. Even if I am still tired and sleepy, I choose to offer myself to the Lord as a sacrifice while singing praise songs to Him, and praying in tongues, and reading His Word.

I am getting recognized now in my work. God is giving me creative ideas. Thank you for your messages, Pastor Steven. God is really helping my family. He has heard the sorrow of my heart and He is changing my situation and making my life better now. He is working through me and in me. Also, it is amazing—I am receiving checks from overpayment I made from my hospital bills. To God be the glory! Thank you for your encouragement. I love you and Pastor Kelly. The Lord Jesus is our portion and reward. God bless!"

R. S.

"While watching you, the spirit of mental illness floated out of me. I fell asleep naturally for the first time in ten-and-a-half years!"

A. P.

"I've watched yesterday's teaching twice already and plan on watching it again. What a blessing this teaching is! It's very relevant for me at this time, and for many others, I'm sure. The assessment from my doctor's appointment today was 'a Perfect Report,' just as you prayed and agreed with me! I continue to praise and thank the Lord for His Word, His faithfulness, and your ministry, which is truly a blessing to me! Thank you for all you do to teach the Word and encourage the body of Christ!"

L. C.

"Pastor Steven, it's so awesome to see the Holy Spirit use you to minister so exactly and delicately to my heart. I love all your messages, but especially, 'When You Realize This Is of God.' What a masterpiece!"

S. R.

"Hey Pastor Steven, my name is A. G. I'm nineteen years old, and I live in Colorado. I was reading my Bible today, and I was reading the book of Job, and I asked God, 'How come there are all these stories about people telling their stories about Jesus and none today?' And before I could finish my sentence telling God I'm going to pray till I get an answer, I heard, 'People like Joel Osteen and Steven Brooks are modern-day storytellers.' I'm very familiar with Joel, but I had never heard of you. I didn't know who you were, so I googled your name, and there you were, the first one to pop up. Steven Brooks, spreading God's Word, working miracles, and telling your story! I sat there and cried as I was reading, shocked with joy that God had answered my prayer and having faith that He would answer me. I will never forget this day! Praise God :-)"

A. G.

"Listening to your internet messages, there is such an anointing and presence of energy that I feel very deflated (ha!) when you go off the air. I dread for you to stop talking! I believe for my entire Hindu family to be saved."

A. A.

"Wow. At the end of the message, when Pastor Steven prayed, I received healing of my neck and shoulders and sinuses, and aches and pains are gone! Glory to God, I feel like I just stepped out of a spa. The Lord is so good. Bless Pastor Steven for sending the Word for me to catch."

T. P.

"Dear Pastor Brooks, my name is Bryan, and I'm nineteen years old. I am from New Jersey. I've been watching your videos for the past two years. I have to say: you're one great storyteller. Your sense of humor really adds to it! I truly, truly appreciate the work you put in for our Lord Jesus Christ!"

Bryan

"Pastor Steven, your ministry helped me through one of the most trying seasons of my life. That God would use you to help me stay the course is something I can't begin to express my gratitude for. I wish I could give you a glimpse at the lifeline that you were to me in some of the hardest times. I wish I could express what God did through you and how I am so grateful for your constancy and ministry. Your messages on Wednesday and Sunday were like life rafts to me: they were convicting, sharp, prophetic, and would literally be the answer to some very, very desperate prayers. Through you, God taught me how to wait and not rush, what excellence looks like, identity, prosperity, and how to walk like a king."

R. Z.

Other Books by Pastor Steven Brooks

To order, please visit our online store at www.stevenbrooks.org.

Working with Angels: Flowing with God in the Supernatural

Standing on the Shoulders of Giants: The Release of Mantles to the End-Time Generation

The Sacred Anointing: The Power to Live Your Dream

Fasting and Prayer: God's Nuclear Power

How to Operate in the Gifts of the Spirit

Manifesting the Blessings of God: How to Receive Every Promise and Provision That Heaven Has Made Available

Printed in the USA
CPSIA information can be obtained
at www.ICGtesting.com
LVHW051742260224
772870LV00049B/1489

9 781637 694862